MORAL CONSISTENCY
WITH LONERGAN'S THOUGHT

Paul K. NYAGA

MORAL CONSISTENCY
with Lonergan's Thought

Domuni-Press

2022

THIS BOOK IS PUBLISHED BY DOMUNI-PRESS
PHILOSOPHY COLLECTION

ISBN: 978-2-36648-175-4
© DOMUNI-PRESS, July 2022

The intellectual property code prohibits copies or reproductions intended for collective use. Representation or reproduction in whole or in part by any means whatsoever, without the consent of the author or his successors, is unlawful and constitutes an infringement of copyright under articles L.335-2 and following of the Intellectual Property Code.

Acknowledgment

It was a great privilege to be awarded a post-doctoral fellowship in Boston College, Massachusetts, USA. Special thanks go to Prof. Patrick Byrne, Mary Elliot, Kerry Cronin and the entire Lonergan Institute for making all the necessary arrangements for my stay in Boston College. I am very grateful for the support of so many competent and generous Lonergan fellows during my stay in 2020/2021. It was a real learning moment for me as I interacted with these Lonergan fellows both online and face to face.

Special thanks to Fr. Francis Preston, SDB, for his wise counsel. Without his careful and critical reading and correction of my text, some of the kernels of wisdom that I gained during my research might have been lost. I am grateful for the time he devoted to ensuring that my work reached the required standard.

I would like to express my hearty gratitude to the Salesians of Don Bosco, the Roman Catholic Congregation to which I belong, and to East African Province (AFE) of which I am a member, for giving me the opportunity to do detailed research at Boston College into Lonergan's thought. In particular, I express my thanks to Rev. Fr. Simon Asira, the Provincial Superior of AFE Province, to Rev. Fr. Augustine Sellam, the Vice Provincial, and Rev. Fr. Eric Mairura, the AFE Provincial Economer, for the financial, moral and spiritual support they provided. I am also very grateful to Rev. Fr. Paul Luseno, the former parish priest of the Nzaikoni parish, for the care and support he gave me during my six months' stay in the parish while I was waiting to receive my US visa. And to all those who helped me and who I may have inadvertently failed to mention, I am forever grateful. May God bless you all.

Foreword

The opening lines of this book by Rev Dr Paul Nyaga were consoling to me. After my own undergraduate studies, as I was preparing for admission to a postgraduate degree in philosophy, I attempted to read Lonergan's *Insight*. I literally slept over the text for days and days, even as I was earnestly jotting down a sentence or two from each paragraph. It seemed a foolhardy effort then. Later, when I did begin my classes, we read extracts from the book as part of the course work. Some "insights" began to emerge! During theology studies, I had an easier reading of *Method in Theology*, but it was not a cakewalk either!

I have relied on Lonergan for insight into epistemological processes such as experience, understanding and judgement. In studying psychology and carrying out research employing empirical data, Lonergan's epistemological framework of generalised empirical method (GEM) has been useful in understanding the three approaches to empirical research, especially in psychology.[1] There are basically three approaches into empirical enquiry, which I present in a reorganised order to make a point.

First-Person Approach: This consists in arriving at conclusions regarding processes in human mind, variations in affective states, and intentions behind behaviour based on data drawn from one's own consciousness. It assumes that if x is what is happening within my mind in a given situation, then x can be extended to understand how another's mind is operating in a similar situation. Conclusions of psychoanalysis have largely relied on this

---

[1] Reddy, Vasudevi. *How infants know minds*. Cambridge, MA: Harvard University Press, 2010, p.7. See also, Sahaya G. Selvam (2015). The methodology of Indian education: An autoethnographic assessment. In J. P. Doss, S. Fernando, & M. C. Antonysamy (eds.), *Empowering education in today's India* (pp. 203-222). New Delhi: Don Bosco Youth Animation - South Asia.

approach. This has given rise to concepts such as defence mechanisms, transference and counter-transference, besides the central concept of the unconscious in psychoanalysis.

Third-Person Approach: Classical positivist methods of data gathering fall under the third-person approach. Here, the researcher assumes a position of a bystander and "objectively" observes and measures the phenomenon under study. The conclusions are based on the objectively recorded data. This approach presupposes that using the same method of data gathering, under the same conditions, two independent researchers will arrive at the same conclusion, regarding the same phenomenon. Physical sciences have relied heavily on this approach. Auguste Comte postulated that the third-person approach can be used in the study of the social phenomenon, and scholars such as Emile Durkheim and Max Weber demonstrated such a possibility in their work. Thus, sociology was born. In psychology, the behaviourist approach has absolutized the third-person approach. While this approach is suitable in the study of the material phenomenon, social constructivists have proposed the second person approach in the study of the social reality.

Second-Person Approach: In this approach, the researcher arrives at conclusions regarding perceptions and experiences of individuals by interacting with them directly by employing participatory methods. Here, the researcher is not just observing the event, but is attempting to experience the event as experienced by the participants of the study. While the first-person approach in research could be subjective in nature, and the third-person approach claims to be objective, the second person approach is intersubjective. In psychology, conclusions in humanistic psychology fundamentally presuppose a second person approach, in understanding motivation and purpose in life. Studies in child development also employ the second-approach.

What Paul Nyaga's work attempts to do in the present book is to apply the generalised empirical method to understanding and assessing moral notions: Golden Rule, Conscience, Natural Law, Virtue Character. Paul's work focuses on the obvious link between epistemology and ethics. Knowing the truth and choosing the good are inseparable processes that involve the intellect and will. In fact, the first chapter of the book traces a brief history of the relationship between knowledge and moral virtue. As the title of the book suggests, the aim of the book is to discuss "the consistency" between the understanding of moral principles and moral choices that one makes. In the words of Paul Nyaga himself, "Moral consistency involves a harmony between what we *know* and what we *do*."

How can the three approaches in empirical research – that is, the methods of arriving at reliable conclusions by means of sense data – be relevant to ethics? I make an attempt to answer this question, using insights from Lonergan as emerging from this book.

The first-person approach in ethics - The Golden Rule: The third chapter of the present book explores the different sources and versions of the Golden Rule: Do unto others, what you would want done to you, or don't do others what you would not want done to you. This principle presupposes that my subjective desires are extendable to knowing others' desires and thus making choices towards their fulfilment. This subjective norm of morality has its limitations. Hence, Paul Nyaga appeals to the formulation proposed by Gensler, "Treat others only as you consent to being treated in the same situation." Here, Nyaga argues that the addition of "in the same situation" brings out a valid meaning of the Rule, thus avoiding the literal application that might lead to moral subjectivity. Nyaga concludes: "When Golden Rule is well articulated and well applied, the result is sufficient moral consistency."

The third-person approach in ethics - Natural Law: The fifth chapter of the present book elaborates the role of natural law in providing a viable moral framework. Considered from the perspective of St Thomas Aquinas, the discourse around natural law is a third-person approach to ethics. According to Aquinas, the natural law contains the basic principles of practical rationality for the human person. And the precepts of the natural law are universally knowable and binding by nature. From this perspective, no one can claim to be exempt from the natural law. However, natural law, even as asserted by Aquinas, assumes divine revelation which makes it inaccessible to a non-believer. In any case, if natural law is considered from within the framework of human nature, then it could provide sufficient level of moral consistency.

The second-person approach in ethics - Conscience and Virtue: Lonergan's critical realist proposal of "dialectic" is basically a second-person approach in arriving at the true and the good. The fourth chapter of the present book examines the role of conscience in moral consistency. And in the first chapter, Paul Nyaga has mentioned almost in passing the role of character which is an expression of virtue, as being very meaningful in the African communal context. I see conscience and virtue as moral components that have a subjective element insofar as they subsist in the individual, but they are also a product of the intersubjective interaction of the individual in their social context. Both conscience and virtue are products of formation. They are outcomes of the "dialectic" between the individual and society. When one acts with clear conscience that is at the same time subjective and objective, there is moral consistency. The dialectic approach in dealing with biases in subjective understanding and judgement of the true and the good marks the process of intellectual and moral conversion. And in the words of Nyaga, "It is only total conversion that can bring about authentic moral consistency."

Could we also suppose that conversion that is synonymous with moral consistency is best expressed in virtue, which is also furnished by some authors as a norm of morality?[2] Virtue-based ethics invites the individual to go beyond mere following of rules to a deeper knowledge of good life and expressing it in a set of habits that improve quality of life for all. Character is nothing but the moral consistency in acquiring and expressing virtues.

Nyaga makes an appropriate connection between character and African conception of morality. According to him, in the African context, "the key word is 'character'. In African morality, the formation of character is of paramount importance. The society has the responsibility to help the individual to mould his/her character. The individual, on the other hand, takes responsibility for his/her character just because he/she has freedom to choose either bad or good habits to live on."

---

[2] MacIntyre, Alasdair. "After Virtue: A Study in Moral Theory [1981]." *London: Duckworth* (2007).

FOREWORD

One of my domains of interest in psychology is positive psychology. This relatively new approach in psychology, since 1998, embraces the three approaches in scientific/empirical enquiry and explores the ingredients of human happiness and wellbeing. Positive psychology considers character strengths which are nothing but concrete expressions of eudemonic virtue, as the ingredients of happiness.[3] This is consistent with the philosophical position of Aristotle and Aquinas. The specific contribution of positive psychology is the plethora of empirical evidence to support the relationship between virtue and happiness. A position that Lonergan would be most comfortable with. Chapter 9 of the present book explores the notion of happiness from Aristotle to Lonergan via Aquinas and others.

Congratulations to my former student and a confrere in my religious order for this thorough work of Lonergan, contextualising him in Africa of the 21st century. Paul makes Lonergan very accessible to a keen reader, without sacrificing the depth of his concepts. This book is a valuable introduction to the thoughts of Bernard Lonergan, and it could be a supplementary reader for a course in moral philosophy in African institutions of higher education. It could also be a worthwhile reading for anyone interested in critical thinking.

Sahaya G. Selvam, SDB, PhD

---

[3] Peterson, Christopher, and Martin EP Seligman. *Character strengths and virtues: A handbook and classification.* Vol. 1. Oxford University Press, 2004.

General Introduction

The first time I came across the *Insight*[4] of Bernard Lonergan, I was extremely puzzled. My first question was, "What was Lonergan's intention when he wrote this voluminous work of about 900 pages?" To be honest, I understood very little of the book when I read it for the first time. It was only later on when I came across Tekippe's *An Introductory Guide to Insight*[5] that I began to understand Lonergan's thought. In his preface, Tekippe states clearly the intention of Lonergan's masterpiece: "between the lines, one reads Lonergan's own ambition to do for the twentieth century what Thomas had done for the thirteenth and what Aristotle had attempted before him: to grasp all human knowing and press it into a masterful synthesis."[6]

What made me fall even more in love with Lonergan's work is what I found in Tekippe's preface. Tekippe writes that one of the most important reasons why a person should engage with Lonergan's work is because it presents a personal challenge. He quotes Socrates' dictum, "know thyself." He reminds the reader that the subtitle of *Insight* is *A Study of Human Understanding*. Here Lonergan is not talking about any abstract understanding; he is not even talking about his own understanding; he is talking about the human understanding of each and every one of his readers.[7] Lonergan's philosophy poses a personal challenge to every reader of *Insight*. In Tekippe's words,

---

[4] Bernard Lonergan, *Insight: A Study of Human Understanding*, Edited by Frederick E. Crowe and Robert M. Doran, Collected Works of Bernard Lonergan, Vol 3, (Toronto: Toronto University Press, 1992). First Published by Longmans, Green and Co. in 1957. All page references to *Insight* refer to the Collected Works Edition. Cited hereafter as *Insight*.
[5] Terry J. Tekippe, *An Introductory Guide to Insight*, (New York: Paulist Press, 2003). Cited hereafter as Tekippe, *Guide to Insight*.
[6] Tekippe, *Guide to Insight*, 2.
[7] Tekippe, *Guide to Insight*, 5.

"it is not some foreign body or even someone else's mind, that one is being invited to study, but one's own mind. The evidence for philosophy is within you."[8] This is an invitation to every reader to engage in self-appropriation as he/she reads through this twentieth century masterpiece. It is written for those who would like to know better the operations of their own mind. This is wonderful. Lonergan states,

> Intellectual mastery of mathematics, of the departments of science, of philosophy is the fruit of a slow and steady accumulation of little insights. Great problems are solved by being broken down into little problems. The strokes of genius are but the outcome of a continuous habit of inquiry that grasps clearly and distinctly all that is involved in the simple things that anyone can understand.[9]

One of the Lonergan's scholars at Notre Dame, David Burrell, undoubtedly spoke for many when he said, "The most important thing about Lonergan is that he liberates you to be - and to trust - yourself."[10] This is clearly the strength of Bernard Lonergan. He liberates the reader. He makes him/her think critically. He makes her/him think for her/himself. He does not encourage his reader to repeat ideas just because they were uttered by some great thinkers in the past. He lets the reader identify all that is happening in her/himself and make a personal judgement that "this is what I am personally experiencing, understanding and judging." It is unfortunate that Lonergan has not yet gained greater popularity. In 1998, in an article on Lonergan entitled *One Hundred Twentieth Century Philosophers*, Hugh Bredin asserted: "Lonergan is regarded by some as having one of the most powerful philosophical minds of the twentieth century, but he is not widely known outside Thomistic circles."[11]

Why have I chosen to write an introduction to the *Insight* of Lonergan? Apart from it being the first book that Lonergan

---

[8] Tekippe, *Guide to Insight*, 19.
[9] *Insight*, 27. See also. Tekippe, *Guide to Insight*, 22.
[10] Fellows of the Woodstock Theological Center, The *Realms of Desire: An Introduction to the Thought of Bernard Lonergan*, (Washington, DC: Woodstock Theological Center, 2011) 3. Cited in Newsweek, April 20, 1970; Time, April 20, 1970, 58-59. Cited hereafter as Woodstock, *The Realms of Desire*.
[11] Woodstock, *The Realms of Desire*, 3.

published, it is the work that inspired me to write this introduction to Lonergan's thought. His cognitional theory and epistemology are the foundations on which this book is constructed. Every chapter of this book starts with a quotation from either *Insight* or *Method in Theology*. Three chapters (two, six and seven) are exclusively on *Insight* and one chapter (eight) is based on *Method in Theology*. The other six chapters end with a thought from Lonergan. At the end of every chapter, I have pointed out 'the contribution of Lonergan'. This explains the reason for the subtitle of this book.

And now a brief introduction to the book itself. The book is entitled *Moral Consistency: with Lonergan's Thought*. This shows that my focus is on moral consistency. Philosophers from antiquity till contemporary times have wrestled with the question of morality. The present work contains ten related chapters, all on moral issues, except chapter two which is about "knowing." The reason for inserting the chapter on "knowing" is to help the reader familiarize him/herself with the notion of knowing as presented by Lonergan. It is the chapter which will guide the reader through the chapters that follow, so that he/she can ask, "How do I know that what I am knowing is correct or incorrect?" And, "How do I reach objectivity in the issue at hand?" Chapter one presents the whole spectrum of moral issues. It is a short historical survey of moral consistency.

Chapter three discusses the "Golden Rule". We explore the genesis of the "Rule" and how it has developed up till today. We will examine different versions of the "Rule". We shall also see the literal meaning of the "Rule" which is often mistaken for the real meaning. Chapter four is on "conscience." It first explores various types of conscience and then discusses the question of the formation of conscience. The teaching of the scholastic thinkers will help us to understand the similarity between *"synderesis"* and "conscience". Chapter five on "natural law" will examine the foundation of moral conscience. "Does human conscience act freely?" This question will lead into chapter six and a discussion on "freedom and responsibility." In this chapter we will educate the reader so that he/she can ask whether he/she is capable of choosing and acting freely on moral issues.

"Can human mind be biased in knowing, choosing and acting?" Chapter seven will help the reader to answer this question. But if the mind can be biased, is there a possibility of redemption? Chapter eight on "conversion" will direct the reader as to how he/she can achieve a three-fold conversion – intellectual, moral and religious. But then the next question arises: "Why should a person strive for moral perfection?" Most moralists agree that happiness is the goal of moral perfection. This topic will be discussed in chapter nine. Can the human person be satisfied with contingent and temporary happiness since it seems that the human soul longs for something more permanent, something beyond the limitations of this universe – the transcendent being? The last chapter, chapter ten, explores the question of God.

Every chapter starts with questions for reflection. These questions are meant to help the reader personally connect with the topic under discussion. He/she has to achieve self-appropriation. At the end of each chapter, there is a case study followed by questions for reflection. This is to help the reader evaluate whether he/she is able to tackle real concrete issues with the heuristic structures provided earlier in the chapter. There is something else, too. At the end of each chapter, there is a section of 'concluding remarks and suggestions. Perhaps this is the unique part of this book. I have tried to make it easier for the reader to grasp the main idea of the chapter at a glance. It is also challenge to the reader to be more critical in his/her reflecting on the ideas brought forward in the chapter. There are also some practical suggestions to help the reader enhance his/her own self-appropriation. I have also attempted to introduce some African thinking into some of the chapters. It was not possible to insert African thinking into every chapter because some topics are to be found more in the domain of Western thinking. But the reader might like to accept the challenge of contributing more African thinking.

This book has three main objectives. First, I identify and then examine eight deliberately chosen moral themes. However, please note, the first theme is a general historical exploration, and the second is exploration of the nature of "knowing". The eight subsequent themes focus on some of the most intriguing issues in the contemporary moral arena. I have tried to give a historical perspective for some of the themes to demonstrate the significance of historicism in handling existential moral issues. Second, since I want to explore Lonergan's thought, and to make him known especially in Africa, I have included his contribution on each of these themes. Third, I want to invite my readers to undertake self-appropriation of each of the themes, in this way helping them achieve self-transformation and enhance their moral consistency.

This book targets the following readers: [a] those who are meeting Lonergan for the first time, or/and those who have little knowledge of him and his thought; [b] undergraduate students of philosophy and theology who are willing to be challenged by the thought of a contemporary philosopher, theologian and economist; [c] all those who believe in a/the Supreme Being (and implicitly non-believers) to strengthen their faith through genuine rational discussion. The topics chosen are universal and open for dialogue with all persons of good will. The language of the book is simple to understand. I have tried as much as possible to be gender-sensitive in all the discussions.

Finally, let me inform the reader about the different branches of ethics. There are four main branches: descriptive ethics, normative ethics, meta-ethics and applied ethics. *Descriptive ethics* deals with what people actually believe (or are made to believe) to be right or wrong. *Normative Ethics* deals with "norms" or sets of considerations on how one should act. Thus, it is a study of "ethical action" and sets out the rightness or wrongness of the actions. It is also called "prescriptive ethics" because it rests on the principles which determine whether an action is right or wrong. Some of the theories of normative ethics are: virtue ethics, deontological ethics and consequentialism. *Meta-ethics* or "analytical ethics" deals with the origin of the ethical concepts themselves. It does not consider whether an action is good or bad, right or wrong. Rather, it asks the question: "What are 'goodness' or 'rightness' or 'morality' in themselves?" It is basically an abstract way of thinking about ethics which scrutinizes and challenges the basic ethical norms. *Applied ethics* deals with the philosophical examination, from a moral standpoint, of particular issues in private and public life which are matters of moral judgment. The four branches are interconnected and each branch needs the others. In this present work the focus in mainly on meta-ethics. However, our "concluding remarks and suggestions" are focused more on normative ethics.

I. Moral Consistency:
A Short Historical Exploration

If a person is to be a philosopher, his thinking as a whole cannot depend upon someone or something else. There has to be a basis within himself; he must have resources of his own to which he can appeal in the last resort...The value of self-appropriation, I think, is that it provides one with an ultimate basis of reference in terms of which one can proceed to deal satisfactorily with other questions.[12]

Questions for Reflection

1. What do you understand by the words "moral consistency"?
2. Have you ever experienced inconsistency between what you *know* and what you *do*?
3. Do you perceive "moral consistency" as a value?
4. Do you think morality is natural to human beings?

Introduction

The term 'consistency' has become a catchphrase in the contemporary sphere of social and human sciences. A good philosopher, as a matter of common parlance, is a thinker who introduces his or her thought, systematically lays down his or her arguments and consistently carries it to its logical conclusion. The thinker has to make sure that there are no contradictions whatsoever

---

[12] Bernard Lonergan, *Understanding and Being: The Halifax Lectures on Insight*, Collected Works of Bernard Lonergan, vol. 5, edited by Elizabeth A. Morelli and Mark D. Morelli, revised and augmented by Frederick E. Crowe with the collaboration of Elizabeth A. Morelli, Mark D. Morelli, Robert M. Doran, and Thomas V. Daly, (Toronto: University of Toronto Press, 1990) 35. Cited hereafter as *Understanding and Being*.

in his or her arguments. In case a contradiction is incurred in the process of argumentation, then it is logical to conclude that this type of work is inconsistent. In judicial matters, lawyers have to be extremely careful in their arguments such that they do not enter into inconsistencies, lest they lose theirs cases as well as their good reputation. A teacher who starts his or her class on time, teaches coherently and ends on time is said to be consistent. A nurse or doctor who attends his or her patients diligently, administers to them with care and concern, and behaves this way consistently throughout his or her life time is highly respected and loved.

In this chapter, we shall not be exploring all types of consistencies. Our main interest is moral consistency. Some moral philosophers have described moral consistency as the absence of contradictions in a person's moral living. This position has sometimes been called the hallmark of ethics. Ethics is supposed to provide us with a guide for moral living, and to do so it must be rational, and to be rational it must be free of contradictions.

Therefore, if our ethical principles and practices lack consistency, we, as rational people, will find ourselves at an enormous and regrettable loss. We shall find ourselves at a crossroads – caught between what we *know* and how we *ought* to live.

We shall now make a short historical exploration of the notion of moral consistency. This topic is vast and we cannot examine the views of all the thinkers from the time of antiquity. We shall take some selected philosophers. These moral thinkers will represent the four great periods in the history of philosophy, namely, the ancient, the medieval, the modern and the contemporary period. After modern period, we shall look into the African notion of morality. In the contemporary period we shall look at the question of self-appropriation as presented by Bernard Lonergan, the key inspirer of this entire book. I will not go into details of morality as presented by these thinkers in this chapter. Some of them will recur in the following chapters.

The Sophistry Period: The Inauguration of the Era of Free Choice

According to Glaucon, (in the *Republic* of Plato) morality is not natural to human beings. It was the Sophists who made the distinction between nature and the human law or convention. In Pre-Sophists era, there was no real developed conception of this distinction. Human beings and all other creatures were believed to be subject to the laws of nature. It was the Sophists who brought about a radical distinction between the world of human beings and that of nonhuman beings. This was the inauguration of the era of thinking, of free choice. The Sophists taught that there is a real distinction between what comes of itself (nature or *phusis*) and what is made from human convention (*nomos*). This was the landmark distinction which caused a kind of revolution in the field of morality.

Now we can understand better why the early Greek thinkers were called the "cosmologists". It was because all their projections were on nature, thus they identified themselves with nature. Many mythological stories in the pre-Sophistic times depict divinity, humanity and nature as one undifferentiated reality. This could explain why the atomists or the early materialists thought that nature was controlled by indivisible atoms. One may ask if, before that distinction was made (as per pre-Sophists), could people be held responsible for their behavior? Could the idea of moral consistency be truly conceived?

John Rawls puts it correctly: when we put nature and human beings together, human beings cannot be held responsible in the contemporary way of understanding the term. He writes:

> They [people] can be held responsible, but only in the way that you hold a dog responsible, without implication that it could have chosen otherwise. People can be praised and admired or condemned and contemned but in the spirit in which natural things are assessed, as you admire a fine horse or throw out a rotten apple with disgust. The vocabulary of evaluation of character, words like *agathos* and *arete* (good, virtue), is applied to animals as it is to people. Dogs can be brave, loyal,

charming, elegant, faithful, perhaps ashamed, but not conscientious, guilt- ridden, in moral conflict, saintly, maybe not sensitive, and it is the first range of terms that is applied to people, not the second.[13]

It was the Sophists who changed this *status quo*. They argued that human beings are not the products of natural processes. They were convinced that there was a clear distinction between nature and human convention. Human beings, unlike other animals, have authority over nature because of their reflective nature. This is the inauguration of the era of free choice. With the introduction of the concept of freedom, human beings can now be held responsible of their free choices. They are deemed accountable for their choices.

Socrates: Knowledge as Virtue

Socrates was a tough critic of the Sophists. As we have seen above, the cosmologists looked at the universe as undifferentiated reality. They did not make a substantive distinction between the human being and the rest of nature. However, the Sophists made this distinction. They speculated about the springs of human action and taught the art of influencing people. Socrates took a large step beyond the Sophists in a humanistic direction.[14]

Throughout history, human beings have searched for knowledge. Socrates, perhaps the most celebrated thinker in the ancient Greek philosophy, claimed to be the most ignorant person at that particular time and space. This earned him great respect and the Delphic Oracle declared him to be the wisest person in entire Greek society. But Socrates knew was not wise, and so he said he had to test the oracle, which drove him to question those purported to be wise: the statesmen, the poets, and people with technical expertise. The 'ignorance' of Socrates was interpreted as 'Socratic irony', and he used it systematically and efficiently to educate the youth of Athens. We know that in all his dialogues, he taught people that the proper

---

[13] G. A. Cohen, *Lectures on the History of Moral and Political Philosophy*, ed. Jonathan Wolff, (New Jersey: Princeton University Press, 2014) 10. Cited hereafter as Cohen, *Lectures*.

[14] Cohen, *Lectures, 24*.

way of living a worth life is to strive for the attainment of knowledge and wisdom.

In fact, in the *Apology* Socrates insists that one has to avoid living the unexamined life because it is not worth living.[15] By this, he meant that a person needs to constantly examine and evaluate his beliefs, values and actions. By seeking to replace opinion based on conventions (*nomos*) with true and certain knowledge based on the using "giving a logical account (*logon tithenai*)." Now the most interesting thing is his identification of knowledge with virtue by using nature (*physis*) as a standard that is independent of convention. For Socrates, only a knowledgeable (i.e., in accord with nature, instead of non-normative convention) person can be virtuous. He goes on to claim that one cannot do wrong if one knows that it is wrong. This means that one cannot err knowingly. To do so would amount to inconsistency. This contention has been greatly challenged by contemporary moral philosophers. There are many people who possess much knowledge on moral issues, yet they deliberately do what they like. On the other hand, we see many people who are not necessarily knowledgeable doing many virtuous actions. There seems to be no necessary relationship between knowledge and virtue.

To understand what Plato means by "knowledge is virtue" we need to read his original dialogues carefully. In his understanding of moral knowledge, Plato makes the distinction between knowledge in general and various degrees of knowledge and opinion. He also makes a clear distinction between different levels of virtue. Plato makes a clear distinction between the cognitive states of knowledge and opinion in his dialogues - *Meno*, *Phaedo*, and *Republic*.

It is after comparing these various degrees of knowledge and various levels of virtues that Plato makes a categorical statement that "knowledge is virtue." [16]

---

[15] *Plato's Apology of Socrates*, 38a.
[16] *Plato's Apology of Socrates*, 20a.

Aristotle: The Principle of Self-Destruction

The fundamental principle held by Aristotle was that a person cannot accommodate a genuine practical contradiction. Similar to his teacher (Plato), Aristotle strongly believed that if an agent knows by deliberating and evaluation (*phronesis*) what he ought to do in relation to the "that-for-the-sake- of-which" (*hou heneka*), the general expression of which is "living well" (*eu zen* or *eudaimonia*), he is obliged to decide (*bouleuethai*) to do (*prattein, praxis*) it. If he does not do it, he enters into a deep inconsistency by taking on habitual vice instead of virtue, that is, there is lack of unity within his soul. This is tantamount to self-damaging. Nobody in his right senses would want to damage or to destroy himself or herself.

People who have sufficient knowledge of basic moral principles are in a better position to attain practical moral consistency. Unfortunately, there is a good number of people in society who do not have access to basic moral principles. One of the most contentious questions asked in the field of morality is, "what is the objective criterion for knowing what is good and what is bad?" This is the question of objectivity of knowing. Chapter two will explicate the notion of knowing. It will help the reader to understand that knowing is a dynamic process. This process can sometimes be complex and painstaking.

However, in some cases, people do not need to go to formal schools to learn basic moral principles. There are many avenues through which moral principles are taught. The prime avenue for learning moral principles is the family. The first and perhaps the most efficient teachers of moral principles are our parents. The primordial question here may be raised: how can an individual reach objectivity if he/she depends on his/her parents for their moral principles? Will relativity not be at play as each family may have a different interpretation of moral values?

Summary of the Ancient Period

There are some very important characteristics of morality to be found in works of ancient moral thinkers. The Greek moral thinkers considered ethics as indispensable for living a good and worthy life.

For them, morality was not a means to achieve an end, but it was being able habitually to choose means in any situation that corresponds to an end that can never become a means. The ancient moralists advocated following reason and not just subjective emotions. Ethics for the Ancients was not just following a set of rules but was based on achieving the end proper to human nature. They strongly believed in natural law (in the sense of *physei* or what is right by nature). The ancient moralists were much concerned with the question of justice in society. They were interested in how to improve the world, how to be a good person (a virtuous person), and how to achieve the true meaning of life in their specific time. This is what amounted to consistency in morality for the ancient thinkers.

St. Thomas Aquinas: Virtue as a Good Quality of the Mind

It was St. Albert the Great who introduced the new era in ethics during the mediaeval period. We have seen above that Aristotle contributed a lot in the perfecting of ethics especially in his *Nicomachean* ethics. However, St Thomas Aquinas completed and perfected Aristotle in a masterly way in his commentary where he developed ethics into a really coherent science. St. Thomas starts his *Summa* with a profound definition of 'virtue' as the good quality of the mind. As a good theologian, he is convinced that the right source of this virtue is God. He states, "Virtue is a good quality of the mind that enables us to live in an upright way and cannot be employed badly – one which God brings about in us, without us."[17] This definition was widely accepted especially during the medieval period. St. Thomas had to put into scrutiny the above definition.

According to Aquinas, virtues have to help the practical intellect to form the right judgement in the pursuance of happiness. This means that for the practical intellect to be right, it has to be in agreement with the right appetite.

The moral teaching of St. Thomas remains ever relevant in all the ages. However, it poses three fundamental challenges especially

---

[17] Thomas Aquinas, *Summa Theologica*, I-II, Q. 5, Art. 8, ad 3, sited in J. Budziszewski, *Commentary on Thomas Aquinas's Virtue Ethics* (Cambridge: Cambridge University Press, 2017) 3.h

in contemporary world. First, in the world inhabited by many anti-religious thinkers and atheists, will the idea of linking God with the virtuous life be truly convincing? Second, when Aquinas defines virtue as the good quality of mind, is he aware that there are many people who claim to have a perfect mind without an idea of what is virtue? Third, following Aquinas' thought, can a non-believer be consistent in his moral behavior without following the precepts of God? These are intriguing questions which will receive some attention in the last chapter on "the question of God".

Immanuel Kant: The Activity of Human Will

One of the most popular and influential moral philosophers in the 18th Century was a German philosopher, Immanuel Kant. According to Kant, the rational will is the ultimate guide for moral law one must completely internalize and generalize the maxim one gives oneself in order for a person to know what matters most and how to act accordingly. Kant goes further to state that this rational will has an innate respect for the moral law not only for the individual self, but also for the whole universe. Kant thus calls this the categorical imperative. The most popular formulation of the categorical imperative is "act only on maxims that you can at the same time will as universal law."[18]

Kant emphasizes that what we do must have a universal intent. The agent has to intend that his or her action could be applicable everywhere, anytime and for everybody. This seems very idealistic and unpractical. However, upon the articulation of what Kant really meant by the maxim, the true and holistic meaning comes to surface.

Kant's morality seems to accommodate all the people of the universe as endowed with good will. He insists on universal acceptability leading to a deep respect for human life. Moral law abides universally in all rational creatures. In fact, he invites us to do what we commonly call "entering into the others' shoes, by asking questions such as, 'how would I do it if I were in his or her position?'" It is similar to Golden Rule, though not identical to it. Kant invites

---

[18] Jennifer K. Uleman, An Introduction to Kant's Moral Philosophy, (Cambridge: Cambridge University Press, 2010), 2. Cited hereafter as Jennifer, *Moral Philosophy*.

humanity to embrace their own free rational human will instead of their inner feelings, as well as the laws of God, since then they would be heteronomous instead of autonomous. When the rational human will is correctly embraced, human beings will know clearly what they ought to do and do it freely at the right time and in the right place. This is rational moral consistency. Moreover, when a person is true to this rational human will, there is no possibility of inconsistency.

It is extremely important to note that Kant does not propagate a selfish kind of morality. The free will is directed towards the good of the other. This is altruism. It is committed to a radically shared rationality. Human beings share a common basis for determining the rational thing to do. That is why he categorically states that we should not treat others as means but as ends in themselves. According to Kant, free rational will is good in itself. It is an end in itself. It does not even need to be compared to other goods in order to judge that it is good (or better than that other kind of good).[19]

This is the fundamental motivation for Kant's moral theory. "A will is free, for Kant, if it determines itself and is not determined by anything else. A will is free, in other words, if it chooses ends, and pursues courses of action aimed at realizing those ends, on grounds that stem from one's own reason, and not on grounds given to it by something or someone external to it."[20] According to Kant, choices, if they are to be real true choices, cannot be dictated by any external rules or standards. It is up to my rational free will to make a choice, otherwise it is not a choice at all! Is Kant advocating total human independence and self-sufficiency? This kind of freedom did not go well with the premodern voluntarists and modern voluntarists who insisted, in the case of premodern voluntarists, that God's will is supreme and has to take precedence, and in the case of modern voluntarists (such as Thomas Hobbes), that will is ultimately arbitrary.

Kant's predecessor John Locke denied that human will is ever free. It is always determined by something else, either nature or calculating reason. Therefore, for Locke, talking about *free will* is

---

[19] Jennifer, *Moral Philosophy,* 8.
[20] Jennifer, *Moral Philosophy,* 9.

nonsensical. On the other hand, Hobbes takes the extreme view. According to Hobbes, there are no obligations whatsoever in the state of nature. Freedom is doing as one pleases.[21]

Kant thinks, then, that if a person is free, he already has all the guidance that he needs within, namely, how to determine what is moral. He strongly believed that if there were no laws of morality, then all actions would be governed by desires and impulses: we would not be free.[22] Well, Kant is probably right when he elsewhere insists that there is a distinction between doing the right thing (e.g., on instinct), and doing the right thing because it is the right thing; the latter alone being conspicuously moral.[23] In conclusion, we can rightly say that free rational will brings about consistency.

African Conception of Morality

Introduction

African societies, just like any other functioning human communities, have systematic, evolved ethical systems. They have ethical values, principles and norms which are meant to guide social moral behavior. Just like African Philosophy, unfortunately, most of the ideas and norms of the African societies have not been given elaborate investigation and clarification, hence there is a need for extensive analysis and interpretation. The African hermeneutical school of thought in the contemporary times has attempted to give interpretation to some of the African fundamental moral ideas and norms.

The Word for 'Ethics' in African Languages

Let us begin with an inquiry into African moral Language. This inquiry will give some insight into the basic conception of the ethics or morality in most of the African societies. It is interesting to see how the word for 'ethics' is understood in various African

---

[21] Cohen, *Lectures*, 110.
[22] Cohen, *Lectures*, 145.
[23] Cohen, *Lectures*, 149.

communities. "It must be noted right from the outset that a substantial number of Sub-Saharan African languages do not have words that can be said to be *direct* equivalents of the word 'ethics' or 'morality'.[24] I will quote word by word the findings of Kwame Gyekye, a renown Ghanaian philosopher and theologian.[25]

    a. When a speaker of the Akan language wants to say, "He has no morals", or, "He is immoral", or "He is unethical", "His conduct is unethical", he would almost invariably say, "He has no *character*" (*Onni suban*).

    b. The statement, "He has no morals", or "He is unethical", is expressed by a speaker of the Ewe language as, *nonomo mele si o* (which means "He has no character").

    c. In Yoruba language and thought the word *iwa* means both character and morality (it also means 'being' or 'nature').

    d. In Igbo language of Eastern Nigeria, the word *agwa*, meaning character, is used in such a statement as "he has no morals" (*onwe ghi ezi agwa).*

    e. In Shona, the language spoken by a substantial majority of the people of Zimbabwe, the word *tsika* means 'ethics' or 'morality'. But when they want to say of a person that "He has no morals", or "He is unethical", they would often use the word *hunhu* which directly means 'character'. Thus, *Haana hunhu* means "He has no character", "He is not moral", "He is unethical".

    f. In South Sotho, a language spoken widely in Lesotho and southern Zimbabwe (Matebeleland), there are no words that are the direct equivalents of 'ethics' or 'morality'. References to the moral or ethical life or behavior are made using words that mean behavior or character. Thus, moral statements such as "he has no morals" or "his action is unethical" will be expressed by words such as *maemo*—which means character or behavior: thus, *maemo a mabe* means "he has a bad character", "his behavior (action) is unethical." When a person behaves (or acts) in ways that are morally

---

[24] Gyekye, Kwame, "African Ethics", *The Stanford Encyclopedia of Philosophy* (Fall 2011 Edition), Edward N. Zalta (ed.), https://plato.stanford.edu/archives/fall2011/entries/african-ethics/. Cited hereafter as Gyekye "African Ethics".

[25] Gyekye "African Ethics".

right, they would say "he has a good character", using the words *lokileng* or *boitswaro*, both of which mean good character or good behavior.

In my own ethnic group (Embu, Kenya), when someone wants to say that "one has no morals" we say "ùyù *ndena mìtugo*" meaning "this one has no character". This is similar to what we have seen above. The central and the most fundamental word for ethics in most of the African societies is 'character'. Let us now see the importance of 'character' in African ethics.

The Centrality of 'Character' in African Morality

In most of the African societies, the person who is generous, kind, honest, sincere, respectful is said to be of good character. In my own community (Embu, in Kenya), if a young person cannot 'give way' (when met on a pathway) to an adult, is said to be of 'bad character'. In most moral evaluations reference is made to the character of a person; thus, character is basic - the crucial element - in Akan, as it is in African ethics generally. *Iwa* (character) is, for the Yoruba, perhaps the most important moral concept. A person is morally evaluated according to his/her *iwa* - whether good or bad. African ethics is, thus, a character-based ethics that maintains that the quality of the individual's character is most fundamental in our moral life.[26] Hence good character is the essence of the African moral system. To make sure that there is a sustained good morals in the society, particular societies (especially in African traditional societies) have to find ways of imparting moral knowledge to its subjects especially when they are young. This, especially in the past, was done through proverbs, folk tales and traditional songs.

Now, having moral knowledge and being aware of moral principles and their implications is one thing. Being able to live in consistency with those moral principles is other thing. Just like any other social groups in other parts of the world, an individual may have sufficient knowledge of the norms of the society, he/she may

---

[26] Gyekye "African Ethics".

willingly accept those norms, but he/she may fail completely to apply them in ordinary live. Gyekye put it rightly,

> In the Akan and other African moral systems such a moral failure would be put down to the lack of a good character (*suban pa*). In other words, the ability to act in accord with the moral principles and rules of the society requires the possession of a good character. Thus, in the context of the activities of the moral life - in our decisions to obey moral rules, in the struggle to do the right thing and to avoid the wrong conduct, in one's intention to carry out a moral duty, the quality of a person's character is of ultimate consequence. It is from a person's character that all his or her actions - good or bad - radiate: the performance of good or bad acts depends on the state of one's character. Wrong-doing is put down to a person's bad character. Thus, the Yoruba maxim (proverb): 'Good character is a person's guard.'[27]

How about the formation of character? Is the person born with 'character' or it is acquired? It is quite clear in African conception of 'character' that a person acquires habits (good or bad) from the society as he/she grows. The society has the responsibility to help the individual to mold his/her character. The individual, on the other hand, takes responsibility for his/her character just because he/she has freedom to choose either bad or good habits to live on. The moral narratives (proverbs, songs, folktales) are meant for individuals to internalize moral values of the society.

The action or deed that led to the acquisition of a newly good habit must be persistently performed in order to strengthen that habit; in this way, virtue (or, good character) is acquired. Over time such an acquired virtue becomes a habit. This is the position of Akan ethics on the development and acquisition of a good (or, bad) character, for this is what the Akan people mean when they say *aka ne ho*, "it has remained with him," "it has become part of him," "it has become his habit." Character is, thus, a behavior pattern formed as a result of past

---

[27] Gyekye "African Ethics".

persistent actions. Thus, moral virtues (excellences of character) or vices arise through habituation.[28]

The Concept of 'Personhood'

Most of the African traditional societies hold that 'personhood' has to be attained as one progresses in life. This is attained in direct proportion to one's participation in communal life. Individuals are given various obligations well defined by the community in which one grows. A Nigerian philosopher, Ifeanyi Menkiti made a concrete statement about moral personhood as he said, "It is the carrying out of these obligations that transforms one from the it-status of early child-hood, marked by an absence of moral function, *into the person-status of later years, marked by a widened maturity of ethical sense - an ethical maturity without which personhood is conceived as eluding one.*"[29]

Let us now have a short analysis of the concept 'personhood' in the African thought. This term carries some ethical presuppositions. According to Gyekye, the word 'person' in the Akan language is *omnipa*. At the same time, the word also means "human being" and the plural form of it means "people". Gyekye further says that in the Akan society, when an individual's conduct very often appears cruel, wicked, selfish ungenerous or unsympathetic, it would be said of that individual that is "he is not a person" (*onnye onipa*).[30] A similar expression is found in Yoruba language in Nigeria. The word *eniyan* in Yoruba means a person. The phrase *Ki i se eniyan* means "he/she is not a human". Such a comment is meant to show that the person has portrayed a behavior, which deprives himself or herself of his/her "personhood'.

The above statements from Akan and Yoruba respectively (*onnye onipa* and *Ki i se eniyan*) underline the conception of moral personhood. In the first place, it is important to note that, even if the individual is said not to be a person, he/she still is acknowledged as

---

[28] Gyekye "African Ethics".
[29] Menkiti, Ifeanyi A., "Person and Community in African Traditional Thought," in Richard A. Wright (ed.), *African Philosophy: An Introduction*, 3rd edition, (Lanham: University Press of America, 1984) 176.
[30] Gyekye "African Ethics".

a human being. This reveals that in African conception, there is a distinction between a human being and a person. One can rightly be a human being without necessarily being a person. In the second place, the above statements reveals that there are certain fundamental norms to which an individual human being ought to display in order to qualify to be a person.

Kwame Gyekye categorically put it this way,

The position here is this: for any *p*, if *p* is person, then *p* ought to display in his behavior the moral norms and ideals of personhood. When the behavior of a human being fails to conform to the acceptable moral principles or standards, or when a human being fails to display the expected moral virtues in his conduct, he is considered to be "*not* a person."[31]

A Humanist Ethic of Ubuntu

We shall now try to understand another important concept in African ethic - the term 'Ubuntu'. It comes from South African Bantu languages. Its root *'ntu'* signifies primal being, person. Magobe B. Ramose has given an analysis of the prefix *'ubu'* and the stem *'ntu'*. According to Ramose, the prefix "evokes the idea of be-ing in general".[32] The *'ubu'* specifies a one-ness, while *'ntu'* specifies a wholeness. Now bringing the two parts together we get that the concept of Ubuntu as a progression into wholeness – the whole being. This is the basis of understanding Ubuntu as an ethical concept.

Over a period, the term has been *'ubuntu'* has received several interpretations. I will discuss shortly the most popular meaning given by Nguni languages of Zulu, Xhosa, and Ndebele in Southern Africa. It is based upon the proverb, *'umuntu ngumuntu ngabantu.'* We also find another proverb in Sotho-Tswana, *'Motho ke motho ka batho babang.'* Both mean, "A person is a person through other persons,"

---

[31] Gyekye "African Ethics".
[32] Mogobe B. Ramose, "The Ethics of Ubuntu," in *The African Philosophy Reader*, Second Edition, eds. P.H. Coetzee and A.P.J. Roux (London and New York: Routledge, 2003), 324. Cited hereafter as Ramose, "Ubuntu".

or "I am because we are."³³ This gives the general meaning of humanness. It also shows how the human being becomes constituted as a being through the community. According to Ramose, this is "one of the first principles of ubuntu ethics is the freedom from dogmatism. It is flexibility oriented towards balance and harmony in relationship between human beings and between the latter and the broader be-ing or nature." [34]

This conception of *ubuntu* contributes to a humanistic foundation from which to base the moral obligation of individuals to the community in which they exist. Thaddeus Metz has attempted to capture some moral judgments by providing a theoretical formulation of an African ethic. He proffers the following definition of *ubuntu* as this theoretical formulation: "An action is right just insofar as it produces harmony and reduces discord; an act is wrong to the extent that it fails to develop community."[35] This theoretical formulation, however controversial it may sound, is a point of discussion. In order to develop such an ethical theory, Metz focuses on *ubuntu* as a central normative principle of sub-Saharan African thought.[36] However, I believe that any authentic ethic should be geared to bringing harmony and tranquility in the society. The 'producing of harmony' and 'reducing of discord' in the society is being morally consistence in the African sense. It is bringing *humanness* into its full potential. And in the African sense, the potentiality of this humanness cannot be actualized fully without the 'other'. This is the humanistic ethic of Ubuntu.

---

[33] Thaddeus Metz and Joseph B.R. Gaie, "The African ethic of Ubuntu/Botho: implications for research on morality," *Journal of Moral Education* 39 (2010) 274.
[34] Ramose "Ubuntu" 326.
[35] Thaddeus Metz, "Toward an African Moral Theory," *Journal of Political Philosophy* 15(3) (2007): 334. Cited hereafter as Metz, "Moral Theory."
[36] Metz, "Moral Theory," 323.

MORAL CONSISTENCY: A SHORT HISTORICAL EXPLORATION

Diagram 1: Personhood in Ecosystem

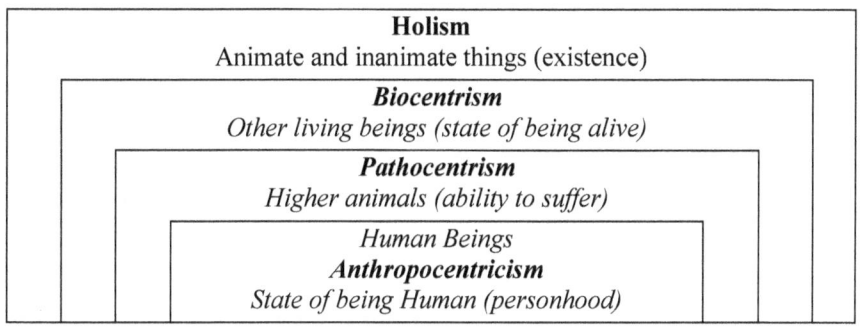

Diagram 2: African Moral Consistency

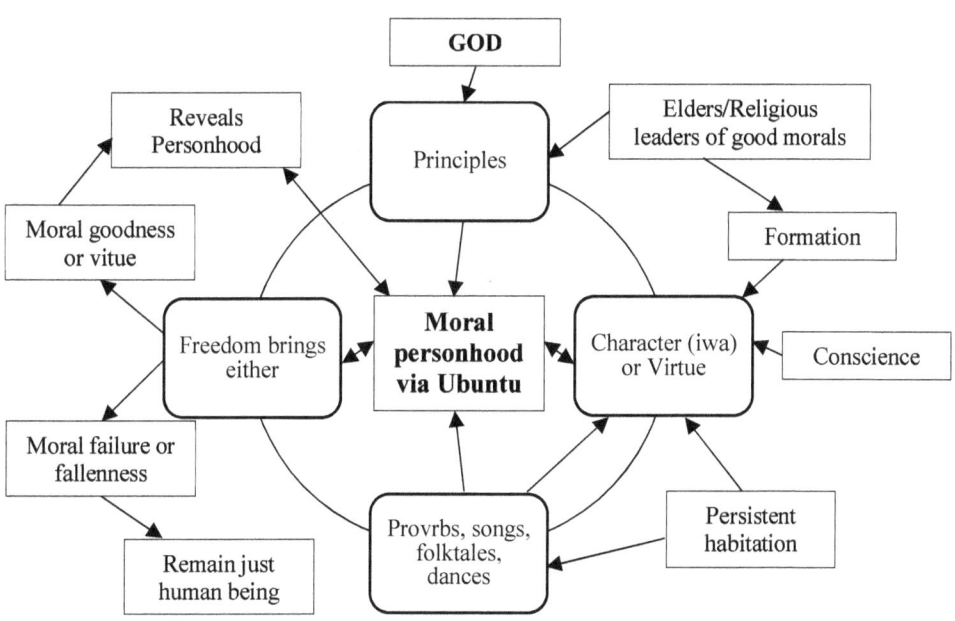

Bernard Lonergan: Self-Appropriation

Introduction

Lonergan has been regarded as one of the finest philosophers and theologians of the 20th Century. However, not many contemporary thinkers have benefited from or acknowledged his intellectual prowess. His work is slowly and steadily gaining popularity in the higher institutes of leaning especially in the seminaries. His masterpiece, *Insight*, reveals the work of genius; it has the potential to transform our way of understanding, verifying and philosophizing. As Brian Cronin puts it, Lonergan's writing is serious, uncompromising, and rigorous.[37] And this rigorousness and relentlessness is exactly what we find in the works of Bernard Lonergan. It is of great importance to know that *Insight* is a series of exercises in self-appropriation.[38]

Self-Appropriation as a Method

Unlike many thinkers who take a particular theme and elaborate it for a specific audience, and formulate their theories, Lonergan has a different approach. He invites the reader to become aware of the inner workings of his or her intellect. Each person has to make his or her own discovery of themselves as knowers and choosers by entering into themselves and exploring their own consciousness. As Cronin puts it rightly, "it is a shift in our way of thinking, a move to a higher perspective, a discovery of our own minds and their potential."[39] This is what Lonergan calls "self-appropriation".

As we start to engage in Lonergan's thought, it is important to understand that he is offering us a method of self-appropriation. According to Lonergan, a method is not a set of rules to be followed meticulously by a dolt. It is a framework for collaborative

---

[37] Brian Cronin, *Foundations of Philosophy: Lonergan's Cognitional Theory and Epistemology*, (Nairobi: Consolata Institute of Philosophy, 1999) 13. Cited hereafter as, Cronin, *Foundations*.
[38] *Understanding and Being*, 17.
[39] Cronin *Foundations*, 14.

creativity.[40] For a method to bear reasonable fruits, it is necessary that many people be involved. This reveals to us that consistency cannot be fully achieved by the efforts of just one individual. It is a collaborative adventure. Lonergan further upholds that a contemporary method would seek to understand how understanding and judgment occurs in the context of modern science, modern scholarship, modern philosophy, of historicity, collective practicality and co-responsibility.[41]

Self-Appropriation as Being Conscious of Oneself

In explaining what happens to a person when she or he is trying to achieve self-appropriation, Lonergan presents three types of 'presences'. It is possible to have a 'presence' like that of desks in a classroom. In this case, the chairs are not aware that they are in the classroom and so they cannot be said to be consciously present to each other. The second sense of 'presence' is being present to someone. This is equivalent to the presence of animals. A cat may enter a room and finds another cat and both become friends. This presence is different from that of the presence of desks in a room. The cats can sense each other, but chairs cannot. This presence can also exist between persons. John can be present to Mary. This presence is different from that of desks in a room. It is also different from the presence of cats to each other. Cats may be aware that they are together but do not seem to be able to raise questions, such as 'why are we together'? At the same time, we can talk of the 'presence' of cats and the 'presence' of John and Mary as 'presence' to a fellow person. They each see or hear each other. There is the third type of 'presence'. To exercise this kind of presence presupposes what Lonergan calls "presence to oneself". In self-appropriation it is this third presence-to-self that is crucial. You are there, and your being there as aware of yourself is the type of presence with which we are concerned.[42]

---

[40] Bernard Lonergan, *Method in Theology,* (Toronto: University of Toronto Press, 1972) xi. Cited hereafter as *Method*.
[41] *Method*, xi.
[42] *Understanding and Being,* 15.

How is it possible to achieve presence of yourself to yourself? Here one cannot take a microscope and look into one's mind. It is impossible to do that. And if one managed to take any complex machine and look into its mind, it would be a matter of having 'presence' of the second type. One would just be looking at oneself. Then one would have to be 'out there' to be present to oneself. But one does not have to be 'out there.' The most important thing here is the subject that becomes explicitly conscious of oneself. This is the fundamental presence.

One can go beyond empirical consciousness – that which can be empirically experienced, and then one attains a heightening of one's self-consciousness. When we are talking to another person, we can be conscious of whether we are understanding, catching the point, or not. Understanding is on the second level of consciousness. Lonergan calls this 'intelligent' or 'intellectual' consciousness.[43]

One can also be present to oneself on the third level of 'rational' consciousness. This occurs on the level of judgement when one asks the fundamental question for reflection: 'Is something true or false'? And one can also go to the fourth level of consciousness - the level of decision and action. Lonergan calls this fourth level 'rational self-consciousness. This is roughly equivalent to what traditionally has been called "conscience," when one asks, "Am I choosing to do what is right or what is wrong"?[44] The answer to this question is found by rational self-consciousness. This is the area we shall try to go deeper in our moral consistency. We want to choose, but it not just choosing, but choosing the right thing. We want to act, but not just any acting, but acting the right way.

Self-appropriation is the process in which a person realizes that when he or she is looking at an object, he or she is not absorbed in the object, he or she is also present to himself or herself.[45] The person becomes aware of his/her awareness. It is awareness looking into his/her own awareness. This is extremely important in moral

---

[43] *Understanding and Being*, 16.
[44] *Understanding and Being*, 16.
[45] *Understanding and Being*, 16.

consistence. Without this awareness, the subject will always be inconsistent.

The Existential Problem in Self-Appropriation

Self-appropriation is an existential challenge. Lonergan reminds the reader that the human decision to undertake self-appropriation is a matter of realizing the authenticity of their existence. And this means that we do not encounter ourselves as instance of a *tabula rasa* (blank state). We carry within ourselves baggage collected over a period of time. Lonergan is chiefly concerned with the kind of "baggage" due to being biased, which we shall discuss later in this book. We already have our goal already operative in us, not merely in terms of our spontaneous intentions of which we may be implicitly aware, but in terms of an explicit awareness of the dynamism of our conscious intentionality, which is at the root of human existence.[46]

Self-appropriation cannot be done mechanically. We do not need to make calculations, use modern scientific instruments for experimental verification, etc. Self-appropriation has to be done in a free atmosphere when the mind is settled and the subject gives free rein to the spontaneously immanent and operative desire to know and to love. A ready-made and ungrounded ideal of what knowledge is supposed to be, may hinder self-appropriation.[47] Another challenge is that when we exercise self-appropriation, we expect quick results. But correct results of self-appropriation may conflict well with already existing explicit ideals, so that another conflict arises.[48] Personal ideals differ from one to another, so that the question of self-appropriation is very personal. In simple terms, Lonergan states accurately that "your ideal of knowledge will govern your attempts at self-appropriation, and unless your ideal is perfectly correct before you start, it will prevent you from arriving."[49]

---

[46] *Understanding and Being*, 17.
[47] *Understanding and Being*, 19.
[48] *Understanding and Being*, 18.
[49] *Understanding and Being*, 21.

Self-Appropriation is a Slow Process

The existential process of self-appropriation is long, slow and tedious. It is a gradual and steady process. Lonergan carefully affirms that "the labor of self-appropriation cannot occur at a single leap. Essentially, it is a development of the subject and in the subject, and like all development it can be solid and fruitful only by being painstaking and slow."[50] By 'development' he means there will be a change or a kind of growth in the subject. And the most important aspect here is the development 'in the subject.' This 'in the subject' is what makes all the difference. If it were the movement 'outside the subject' meaning 'subject reaching the object,' perhaps it would be easy. It is easier to 'look-outside-there' than scrutinizing one's 'inner presence-to-self.' It requires explicit and conscious effort for the subject to heighten one's consciousness. And the more deeply subjects enter into themselves, the better and the closer they come to themselves. Then result is more likely to be a sincere authentic consistency in the moral life of the subject.

Self-Appropriation as Self-Discovery

We are performing acts of experiencing, understanding and judging all the time. Sometimes we are expressly conscious of these acts, while at other times we are not. It is a matter of isolating these activities when they occur in a relatively pure form and becoming explicitly aware of them. Lonergan makes this clear when he says:

> the point is to discover, to identify, to become familiar with, the activities of one's own intelligence; the point is to become able to discriminate with ease and from personal conviction between one's purely intellectual activities and the manifold of other, 'existential' concerns that invade and mix and blend with the operations of intellect to render it ambivalent and its pronouncements ambiguous.[51]

Now, to be able to discriminate between one's purely intellectual activities and other existential activities, one needs to be

---

[50] *Insight*: 17.
[51] *Insight*, 14.

in purely intellectual pattern of experience. It is an invitation to an intellectual journey. It calls for personal effort, involvement and reflection. It is not easy to remain in this pattern of experience. One finds oneself often drifting to other patterns of experience (biological, aesthetics, dramatic), which drive and guide one's daily activities. Here one needs to be directed by a pure detached spirit of inquiry. It is a critical spirit in one's cognitional structure. The intellectual pattern of experience generates a kind of flexibility that makes it a ready tool for the spirit of inquiry.[52] Entering and remaining in this pattern of experience depends on a variety of factors. These factors include external circumstances such as experience of life and training, age, natural giftedness etc. Personal effort in order to be in this pattern of experience is of paramount importance.

Importance of Self-Appropriation

Now one may ask, what is the importance or value of self-appropriation? When we achieve self-appropriation, will it be of any benefit to our daily living? Or is it merely to satisfy our intellectual curiosity? Will self-appropriation help to guide our moral consistency? The quest for self-appropriation, as seen above, is overwhelmingly significant. Self-appropriation means what we undergo when we make cognitional processes clear to ourselves. In the first place, one experiences oneself as experiencing, understanding, and judging. Secondly, one understands oneself as experiencing, understanding, and judging. In the third place, one confidently affirms oneself as experiencing, understanding, and judging. It is after this affirmation one can proceed to make a meaningful and appropriate judgement of value. This is already a fundamental value in self-knowledge. Self-appropriation, as Lonergan puts it, "provides one with an ultimate basis of reference in terms of which one can proceed to deal satisfactorily with other questions."[53] Through self-appropriation, the subject thinks and reflects and ultimately appropriates the most important foundation for his/her philosophy in general and morality in particular. Moreover, this becomes the basis for his/her consistency in morality.

---

[52] *Insight*, 213.
[53] *Understanding and Being*, 35.

The subject is now able to reflect and come out with his/her philosophy. He/she is able to formulate his/her moral standing. He/she is able to defend his/her actions. This is truly the significance of self-appropriation.

I would like to end this first part of self-appropriation with what Patrick H. Byrne conceives as true meaning of self-appropriation. According to Byrne, "self-appropriation does not teach people how to perform the activities of knowing, valuing, or deciding. Rather, self-appropriation begins from experiences of knowing, valuing, and deciding that people have been performing all along. [...] These activities of knowing, valuing, and deciding are also activities of trying to live ethically (and even trying to avoid ethical living) that people have been doing for a long time, well before anyone ever embarked upon any explicit guided exercises in self-appropriation. But self-appropriation does add 'something extra': it adds intensified awareness, better understanding, deeper appreciation, and strengthened commitment to the performance of what is best in the activities that people have been performing all along."[54] This is exactly the goal of this book. If the reader after reading this book will have attained some more knowledge of the performance of his/her activities of knowing, valuing, deciding, and loving then he/she will have achieved the goal of this book.

Lonergan's Contribution

1. Unlike many philosophers who keep on telling us what to do and what not to do, Lonergan's approach is quite different. He invites each one of us to become aware of the inner workings of our intellect. We have to make our own discovery of ourselves as knowers and choosers by entering into ourselves and exploring our own consciousness. It is a conscious shift in our way of thinking, a move to a higher normative perspective, a discovery of our own minds and their potential.

---

[54] Patrick H. Byrne, *The Ethics of Discernment: Lonergan's Foundations for Ethics*, (Toronto: University of Toronto Press, 2017) 32-33. Cited hereafter as Byrne, *Discernment*.

2. By inviting us to self-appropriation, Lonergan offers a critical and reflective method to each one of us. We need to invite other people to assist us in our self-discovery. Their expertise might be of great importance.

3. Through self-appropriation, we engage in thinking and reflecting in depth and ultimately appropriating the most important foundation for our philosophy in general and morality in particular. Moreover, this becomes the basis for our consistency in moral living.

4. And finally, as Byrne has put it strongly above, self-appropriation adds intensified awareness, better understanding, deeper appreciation, and strengthened commitment to the performance of what is best in the activities that we have been performing all along.

Concluding Remarks and Suggestions

1. We have introduced the topic on "moral consistency." It is important to see how philosophers in the course of history debated on the issue of morality. It is equally important to note that all serious philosophers had to give their moral stance. This portrays the significance of morality in any given society.

2. From the existential point of view, moral responsibility (status of morally deserving praise, blame, reward, or punishment for an act or omission in accordance with one's moral obligations) defines our being.

3. Theories and ideas of philosophers help in building collective moral responsibility (c.m.r refers *in most contexts* to both the causal responsibility of moral agents for harm in the world and the blameworthiness that we ascribe to them for having caused such harm). Individual moral responsibility is as a result of how we articulate, personalize and appropriate some of these ideas.

4. There is much we can learn from the African conception of morality. The key word is "character." In African morality, the formation of character is of paramount importance. The society has the responsibility to help the individual to mold his/her character. The individual, on the other hand, takes responsibility for his/her

character just because he/she has freedom to choose either bad or good habits to live on.

5. Lonergan has reminded us that it is only through self-appropriation that we can become better human beings, and relate in a more meaningful way with other human beings. Self-appropriation is not an option but an obligation for holistic growth in self-love and love of humanity.

6. Having heard views on moral consistency from various thinkers, we suggest the following:

   a. That as Socrates believed on self-examination of moral life, it a moral obligation for each one of us to make critical evaluation of our personal moral lives.
   b. Self-critical evaluation will unearth some of the deep-seated moral issues which need urgent attention. We should not shy off in seeking for moral and psychological help where necessary.
   c. We need to create an open and free atmosphere which will enhance other people to interact with us more easily.
   d. We need also to reach out to others who may be struggling with keeping their moral consistency.

Chapter two will help us familiarize with the notion of knowing and how we reach objectivity as presented by Lonergan.

Case Study 1: The Question of Identity

Identity is one the most fundamental philosophical questions that human beings struggle to grasp. However, the more a person seeks to grasp his/her identity, the more he/she realizes its elusiveness. People have gone to the extent of terminating their life, just because they could not understand their real selves. Consider the following case.

John wakes up one morning, totally confused and he runs towards the family's coffee plantation. There he decides to hide himself. His friend Robert happens to pass that way and he sees John. Robert calls John three times, but John decides not to respond. Robert goes closer to John, looks closely at him, shakes him, but in vain.

Robert then runs to John's home and calls his mother. He returns with John's mother and when John sees his mother, he starts crying. A somber mood is created.

John's mother realizes that her son is depressed. She holds her hand out to him and with the help of his friend Robert, all three reach the house. A conversation begins: "Mum, the other day I asked you about my dad's disappearance and you refused to answer me. Yesterday I began a conversation about your refusal to let me go for the interview for the job on space exploration and you wouldn't let me express my desire to apply for that job. The only thing you keep telling me is that I am not mature enough to make life's decisions. If my dad were here, I am sure he would understand me better. You do not understand what I am going through. I will leave this house and then you will never be able to find me. I'm really fed up with the way you treat me." John's mother listened carefully, and the only reply she made was, "I'm sorry, my son, that I have never taken you seriously. Let's sit down and talk."

Questions for Deliberations

1. What do you think is the source of all John's troubles?
2. When John hides himself in the coffee plantation, has he really 'hidden' himself?
3. Can self-appropriation be of help to John?
4. Who needs more "self-appropriation", John or his mother? And why?
5. Is John justified in thinking that his dad could have assisted in alleviating all his troubles?
6. Do you find any moral consistency in John's argument?

II. Thinking, Knowing and Objectivity

Once those ambiguities are removed, once an adequate self-appropriation is effected, once one distinguishes between object and objectivity in the world of immediacy and, on the other hand, object and objectivity in the world mediated by meaning and motivated by value, then a totally different context arises. For it is now apparent that in the world mediated by meaning and motivated by value, objectivity is simply the consequence of authentic subjectivity, of genuine attention, genuine intelligence, genuine reasonableness, genuine responsibility.[55]

Questions for Reflection

1. Have you ever known something with certainty?
2. What was your state of mind when you knew something?
3. What made you know that you reached knowledge?
4. Do you experience some kind of process when you are knowing?

Introduction

Moral consistency involves a harmony between what we *know* and what we *do*. The greatest challenge is in our knowing. How do we know that we have reached knowledge? How do we know that we have reached not just any knowledge, but a correct knowledge? How do we reach the affirmation that we have truly known? It is now important to familiarize ourselves with human knowing. This chapter will briefly discuss "knowing" as illustrated by Lonergan in the

---

[55] *Method*, 265.

Insight. In *Insight* (which comprises of twenty chapters), Lonergan poses four fundamental questions. First, "what am I doing when I am knowing?" This yields cognitional theory (Chapters 1-10). Second, "why is doing that knowing?" This is the epistemological/objectivity question (Chapters 11-13). The first eight chapters explore human understanding, while the other five reveal how correct understanding can be discerned.[56] Third, Lonergan investigates the metaphysical question which asks, "what do I know when I do that?" (Chapters 14-17). The last question is methodological which asks, "what/how therefore should we do?" (Chapters 18-20, the method in doing ethics and the method in approaching the question of God). Our main interest in this chapter is the first and the second questions. This will be a brief Summary of Lonergan's cognitional theory and epistemology. Apart from *Insight*, we shall also use other works of Lonergan, just to reinforce his thought in *Insight*.

Part I: Cognitional Theory (Thinking)

The Term 'Cognition'

It is surprising that the term 'cognition theory' is not found in the famous encyclopedias of Philosophy such as *Routledge Encyclopaedia of Philosophy* and *The Ecyclopaedia of Philosophy* edited by Edward Craig and Paul Edwards respectively. However, the term 'cognition' is well defined in *Webster's Third New International Dictionary*. It comes from Latin word *cognoscere* which means the act or process of knowing in the broadest sense. Specifically, it means an intellectual process by which knowledge is gained about perceptions or ideas.[57] Many authors do not distinguish between cognition theory and epistemology. It is Lonergan who makes such clear distinction in *Insight*.

---

[56] *Insight*, xx.
[57] Philip Babcock Gove, ed. *Webster's Third New International Dictionary*, (Springfield: G & C Merrian Company, 1969) 440.

The Eureka Experience

Lonergan opens his great masterpiece (*Insight*) by presenting a dramatic event - a true story of a Greek mathematician, Archimedes, who was given an important task by king Hiero. King Hiero desperately wanted to find out whether his crown was made of pure gold or if it had been mixed with other baser metals. This might have given Archimedes sleepless nights. Perhaps the genius had already given up finding a solution, and probably this was why he decided to go to relax in the Syracuse bath-house. That was where the moment of insight occurred. It was with great relief that he rushed from the baths of Syracuse crying cryptically "Eureka!" which in Greek means "I have found it." At last, this extraordinary genius had found the solution to King Hiero's dilemma. It was during a quiet relaxed moment, as he was taking a bath that the overflowing water gave Archimedes the insight he needed – weigh the crown in the water.[58] This is what Tekippe calls the "aha!" moment in which all the clues fall into place.[59]

In most cases, we find that insights come not during times of ordinary business, but when we are relaxing, when the mind is cool, calm and not perplexed by worries caused by this created universe. What follows is the rigorous work of making a formulation and using already existing principles to come up with something new and original. What happens for many people is that after some time struggling with a particular problem, they give up and start something new altogether. This may cause them to miss a golden opportunity for a new insight.

Moments of insight may be vivid or less vivid. They are significant moments of transition – from lack of understanding to understanding. They are moments of grasping a new truth.

Lonergan invites us not to learn insights from others, but rather for each one of us to recognize similar experiences in our own process of knowing. This he calls "self-appropriation" which we have discussed briefly in Chapter One above. Self-appropriation is

---

[58] *Insight*, 27.
[59] *Guide to Insight*, 14.

basically not a learned process, otherwise it would be a contradiction in terms.

We can be assisted in doing "self-appropriation." We may think when we talk of insights, that they mean dramatic moments like that of Archimedes. That is not always the case. Brian Cronin gives us some simple examples of moments of insights when he writes:

> For most of us the experience of insight is routine, taken for granted, not adverted to. But we are understanding whenever we are reading, speaking, listening to a lecture, taking notes, driving a car…Our interest is not in learning mathematics, but in identifying the experience of understanding.[60]

The key word here is "identifying." Are we able to identify our experience of our knowing? Can we identify our experience of experiencing? Can we identify our experience of understanding? Can we identify our experience of reaching judgment? Cronin explains the reason of starting every chapter of his book, *Foundations of Philosophy,* with exercises (and I have adopted similar method in this book). He says that these exercises are designed to make the reader stop and think, to provoke the experience of puzzlement. Cronin suggests, "Do some puzzle and, having found the solution, reflect back on the mental processes involved in solving it. What images did you use? What figures did you write down? What led you astray? What blocked you from understanding? What was the clue that helped you to solve it? Where did the insight come from?"[61]

Now let us go back to the notion of insight. The "insight" of Archimedes reveals the following about an insight:[62]

1. The tension of inquiry is relaxed
2. It comes suddenly
3. It is a function of inner conditions
4. It is a fulcrum between the concrete and the abstract
5. It becomes habitual

---

[60] Cronin, *Foundations* 65.
[61] Cronin, *Foundations* 65.
[62] Cf. *Insight,* 28-31.

Let us now have a brief explanation of the above aspects of the emergence of an insight.

Relaxes the Tension of Inquiry

It is unquestionable that every "homo sapiens", every thinking being, when all other appetites are stilled, and the body has achieved a moment of free relaxation, has a greater likelihood of grasping a truth which he/she had never thought of before.

The desire to know, the desire to find the causes of something, the desire to explain things is strong when one is free from other biological needs. This desire can keep people locked in their rooms for hours on end. It can make a person forget everything else. It can be so intense as to lead to mental breakdown. However, there comes a moment when this tension is released. And this is the moment of insight.

The main difference between human beings and animals is that human beings are naturally endowed with the capacity to ask questions. This propensity enables human beings to move from one stage of development to the next. Advocates of the rights of animals (who say that they have rational powers) need to explain why there is little if any development in their lives. Monkeys continue to jump from one tree to the next in their search for food in the same way they have done for centuries. Birds continue to make similar nests as they have done from the moment of their creation. The mongoose continues to live in similar holes from one day to the next. This is not the case with human beings.

The critical spirit in man (to know and to understand) is evident right from childhood. A child is curious to know why her father has a beard and why her mother has none. She is eager to know where the children come from. The manner in which she asks questions is more spontaneous. She does not need to formulate questions before she asks them. However, as she grows up, she learns how to set and formulate questions in order to get better answers.

Philosophy started in wonder. The first cosmologists wondered about the *urstoff* of the universe. They wondered about the ultimate cause of all that is. The eros of the mind took them to the heights of critical reasoning. But did they get all answers to their enquiries? Did they stop wondering after some time? What is at stake here is that, in their wonder after some days of tension, they succeeded in achieving an insight, a moment of understanding. Now we find that all the questioning of man is solely for the sake of understanding. Moreover, before we reach that point of grasping a point, there is some tension in us. This tension is very relevant for the attainment of insight. It should neither be ignored nor be subverted.

Comes Suddenly

Insight is reached not by learning rules or by studying a complicated methodology. We do not need lectures on how to gain or capture an insight. However, because people have different gifts, some take longer than others to achieve an insight. Nevertheless, the fact remains that insight comes suddenly and in most cases at a time when least expected.

It is a known fact that because of their nature human beings keep on questioning. However, the answers do not follow immediately. Some answers may arise after a short time, while others may take much longer to emerge. This depends on the type of question posed, (some questions are simple while others are more complex) and the giftedness of the enquirers. One person may struggle with a certain issue and reach a point of despair, or he may abandon the struggle all together. If the problem was so clear, a solution may sometimes be reached during moments of sub-consciousness. Psychologists have shown that the brain works even when one is asleep. And at a certain moment, when one does not expect it, all of a sudden an insight emerges. For Archimedes it was during a moment of relaxation. But this is not always the case. An insight can also emerge when one is occupied by the cares of this world.

A Function of Inner Conditions

At the time of Archimedes, many people visited the baths of Syracuse, yet no one else grasped the principles of hydrostatics. Nevertheless, all those who bathed there felt the water either cold or warm. These are the outer circumstances. For insight, the inner conditions are crucial. Lonergan is of the opinion that to some extent, insight depends upon native endowment. One also needs to be constantly alert to oneself and ever curious to know.

In the learning process, environment plays a very vital role. If a child is brought up by parents who are both mathematics teachers, that child stands a great chance of becoming a mathematician. Taken literary, this example seems to indicate out conditions. But the external conditions (the fact of having parents who teach mathematics) can be turned into inner conditions (parents engansing thier child into serious mental exercises in mathematics). The environment here is the inner conditions of the mind. Cronin explains what this means:

> Primarily, it means to be continually asking questions; to be manipulating the data in the direction we think the solution lies; to be looking at the problem from different angles, dragging up new images, testing examples, remembering similar situations, exploring possibilities, trying analogies, starting again when we reach a dead end.[63]

A Fulcrum between the Concrete and the Abstract

Going back to the example of Archimedes, the solution to the problem of King Hiero was concrete. The king had to weigh the crown in water. However, that was not the point of interest. The significance of the whole procedure was the discovery of the abstract formulation of the principles of displacement and of specific gravity. Thus, the significance and relevance of insight went beyond any concrete problem. Hence, insight is the mediator, the hinge, the pivot.

Usually our minds oscillate between concrete and abstract realities. Thinking is abstract, but our thinking is provoked by real concrete situations in the world. Unlike the mind of animals, the human mind is able to create images which are not there in reality. This is possible because the mind is capable of receiving different

---

[63] Cronin *Foundations*, 71.

images and combining them, and the result may be something which does not exist. An image is a sensible presentation.[64] The mental power of combining images in the abstract makes insights possible.

Secondly, we have ideas. We have already seen that images are concrete and particular, and thus they provide material for imagining. Ideas on the other hand are abstract and universal. Mathematical formulas are abstract and universal and thus they are ideas. Lonergan demonstrates that ideas are the products of intelligence.

Now one may ask, what is the difference between ideas and concepts? Cronin explains clearly that concepts are ideas that are formulated explicitly and expressed in words or symbols or definitions.[65] A person may have mere bright ideas, but so long as they are not yet formulated, they remain bright ideas. But once they are formulated, they become concepts.

What is our normal experience of the process of knowing? Can we separate images from ideas? Usually they work hand in hand. It is almost impossible to teach little children without images. Children want to see what they hear. In this way, learning becomes not only possible but easier. In adults, fewer images are needed because their level of conceptualization is higher. We find ourselves using live examples to explain things. This is because people are prone to make mental images every moment they enter into thinking.

It Becomes Habitual

At first, an insight might be very difficult to achieve. We may tend to get frustrated and give up and many people have lost great opportunities because of impatience. Yet, once an insight is achieved, once it is understood, the rest can be repeated almost at will. This is precisely what makes learning possible. Insights add into insights. The result is the accumulation of knowledge.

How is it that some things we learnt when we were little children are still fresh in our memories? What makes it possible for us to learn many subjects and still remember a great many things at

---

[64] Cronin *Foundations,* 72.
[65] Cronin *Foundations,* 74.

the end of the semester? It is simply because what we grasp well goes into the habitual texture of our mind. Some things which we learnt in the past can still be recalled at will. Insights are able to capture those things and retain them for future remembrance. And this is what makes learning possible. If this was not the case, then we would remain stuck, unchanging throughout our lives. Perhaps this is why animals repeat the same things day in, day out. There is no intellectual development in them, no new things, no creativity.

How an Insight Emerges

Lonergan gives an example using the emergence of the definition of a circle. In examining this emergence or genesis, we will try to become more sharply aware of how an insight arises. This is the definition of a circle: a locus of co-planar points equidistant from a center.[66] One may ask, how does this definition originate? The starting point is an image. Let us take an image of a cartwheel, and let us ask the question: why is this wheel round?

We have noted earlier that questions must be accurate and definite, and so the next step is to limit the question. We are not interested in the purpose for which the wheel is round, or in the utility of round wheels; neither are we interested in those who made the wheel round, or in the tools they used: such questions would lead us away from the wheel itself. We are interested in the reason for the "roundness" of the wheel, the immanent reason for its roundness.

At this point a suggestion might arise: maybe the wheel is round because its spokes are equal. This is the clue. But is it the answer? No, because the spokes could be sunk unequally into the hub, or else the wheel could be flat between the spokes.

Lonergan insists that we have to push the clue further. If, for example, the hub could be reduced to a point, and the rim and the spokes to lines, and if we had an infinity of equal spokes, we would come to the conclusion that the *rim* would have to be perfectly round.

[6666] *Insight*, 31.

Here, according to Lonergan, is the moment of insight. Once this is achieved, the definition can be formulated.

Higher Viewpoints

One may pose a question: is there development in insight? So far, we have been looking at single insights especially in related fields. However, this is not always the case. In some instances, insights may combine, cluster, and coalesce into the mastery of a subject.[67] Further insights may arise. How does revision of the previous position come about? This is when insights develop and the shortcomings of the previous positions come to the surface. This may lead to new definitions. Such a complex shift in the whole structure of insights may be referred to as the emergence of a higher viewpoint.

We have outlined the heuristic structure, leading from questions to correct answers. By this means we get an answer to one particular, limited and specific question, but automatically, further questions arise. They might be questions seeking deeper understanding, or they might be seeking more information about other topics. If they are aiming at a deeper understanding, they are usually aimed at a higher viewpoint.[68]

A higher viewpoint presupposes a set of insights at a lower level of generality. We question, study and eventually correctly understand some particular matter or data; we move to related matters; ideas accumulate, similarities are noted. Each individual insight unfolds according to the characteristics already identified. In its way this is valid, answers to the questions raised pass into the habitual texture of the mind.[69] But at a certain point the further question will arise as to how this aggregate of insights relate together. Is there an organizing act of intelligence that can see how they fit together? At this stage, the data for the further insight are precisely the set of earlier insights, which have already been achieved. What is sought is the principle of unification which will establish what these insights have in common, and how they differ; what is sought is an

---

[67] *Insight*, 38.
[68] Cronin *Foundations*, 180.
[69] Cronin *Foundations*, 181.

insight into insight, or more precisely, a higher viewpoint. The higher viewpoint is characterized by its generality, its simplicity, its greater exactitude and precision.[70]

Inverse Insights

We have already noted that we have two kinds of insights: direct and inverse insights. We have already discussed direct insights to some extent. While direct insights grasp the point, or see the solution, or come to know the reason for something, inverse insights apprehend that there is no point, or that the solution is to deny a solution, or the reason is that the rationality of the real admits distinctions and qualifications. This sounds strange and seems to be an apparent contradiction. But we need to note that to deny intelligibility already reached, is not the reverse of inverse insight; it is merely the correction of an earlier direct insight, the acknowledgement of its shortcomings, the recognition that it leaves problems unsolved. But to deny an expected intelligibility is to run counter to the spontaneous anticipations of human intelligence; it is to find fault not with answers but with questions.

Cronin gives several examples of different sets of insight which we have made reference to earlier. One of the examples stands out more than the others and we shall consider it. Suppose you take a textbook and start reading it and you reach a point when you realize that you can't understand anything. You start assuming that the author is too bright for you. You continue reading, determined to understand the mind of the author, yet after a while you still fail to understand anything. But slowly and painfully you realize that the author is confused, that he presents his material badly and is trying to impress by using big words and obscure ideas. For sure he does not know what he is talking about. Cronin says that this is the whole point. You have now grasped the mind of the author and his book. At this moment, you do not understand the message the author is trying to communicate, but you now understand that he has no intelligible message to share. And this is an insight, a new strange kind of

---

[70] Cronin *Foundations*, 180.

insight.⁷¹ This is an inverse insight which is quite different from a direct insight. A direct insight grasps what is there, while inverse insight grasps what is not there. We can define an inverse insight as an insight into the absence of an expected intelligibility.⁷²

A classical example of an inverse insight is Newton's first law of motion. Spontaneously we expect that a moving body will come to a halt unless there is some force or energy that keeps it moving. But the law states that a body continues to be in a state of uniform motion in a straight line unless disturbed by some external force. In other words, if a body is moving, it will keep moving unless prevented from doing so; there is no force or energy that keeps it moving. We expected to discover some such force or energy; but we discover that there is no such force or energy.

We may note the following points: first, there is data; second, there is a question - we expect an intelligibility; third, there is an insight; fourth, the insight grasps the point that there is no point to be grasped. Consequently, the intelligibility that we expected is denied.

The conceptual formulation of a direct insight affirms an intelligibility, though it may deny expected empirical elements: thus, for example, a point can be understood, but it cannot be imagined. An inverse insight on the other hand affirms empirical elements (uniform motion) but denies expected intelligibility (a cause of motion).

Inverse insights must be distinguished from corrections of previous direct insights. Sometimes we get an insight, and then later on correct it. This is not an instance of inverse insight; it is merely the correction of a previous direct insight. We have inverse insights when we are expecting some intelligibility, and finally grasp that there is no intelligibility to be grasped. When we correct previous direct insights, we find fault with the answers. When we have an inverse insight, we find fault with the questions.⁷³

Thus, inverse insights regularly tend to be of great significance. Newton's discovery served to transform mechanics: the Aristotelians

---

⁷¹ Cronin *Foundations*, 124.
⁷² Cronin *Foundations*, 127.
⁷³ *Insight*, 44.

were preoccupied with motion, but with Newton, the focus turned to acceleration (i.e., to *change* in motion). The amazing subsequent developments and the fruitfulness of mechanics bear testimony to the value of Newton's discovery.

Heuristic Structure[74]

Archimedes used the word *heurisko* (eureka) which was translated as "heuristic" in English. Lonergan applied the word to describe the strategy of moving from question to insight.[75] Heuristic is a tool for finding out, a devise which helps a person to find out something. It gives light to the one who is searching. This tool is inherent in each one of us. It is the tool which aids self-appropriation. A heuristic structure is therefore a tool for discovery. It is named a 'structure' because it is spontaneously operative even before we study and formulate it.

We have already seen earlier that knowing is a process of moving from the known to the unknown. Mathematicians will call the unknown, which they are searching for, "x". And they will say, let the number be x. The empirical sciences adopt a similar approach. Instead of calling the unknown "x", they call it the "nature of".

Every science requires a method. Lonergan defines method in the simplest way possible when he says that method consists in ordering means to achieve an end. Then he goes on to ask, 'how will means be ordered to an end when the end is knowledge?'[76] He suggests the answer to this question is the heuristic structure which works like this: name the unknown, work out its properties, use these properties to direct, order and guide the inquiry.

Cronin argues that there is a structure in the mind which enables us to move from images to ideas, from the sensible to intelligible, from the known to the unknown.[77] This is the heuristic structure. He goes onto say that a heuristic is a device that helps us to

---

[74] *Insight*, 57-92.
[75] Terry J. Tekippe, *What is Lonergan up to in Insight?* (Collegeville: The Liturgical Press, 1996) 59.
[76] *Insight*, 68.
[77] Cronin *Foundations*, 84.

find something, to move from the unknown to the known, and that it gives direction to our search. It is an anticipation of the known while it is still unknown. Further, he says that heuristic guides our questioning of data to a fruitful and correct understanding.[78]

Part II: Epistemology (knowing) and Objectivity

Making a Transition

Now we need to make a transition. Our short discussion has been centered on knowing as an activity. We have been looking at the facts of knowing in our own conscious activity. We considered the activities of sensing, hearing, tasting and smelling. We have considered activities of understanding and those of judging. We have tried to give accurate accounts of these conscious activities. We have seen that these activities are not just separate activities, but they coalesce into a unity as interrelated dynamic parts in cognitional structure. As we have seen in chapter one, the method of self-appropriation urges each one of us to pay attention to our experiences of performing these activities in our conscious selves. In doing this, it becomes relatively easy to grasp the true relationship between subjectivity and objectivity, instead of falling for the fallacies of the "subject/object split" and the so-called "problem of the bridge."

Human Beings Desire to Know

In *Insight*, Lonergan argues that "Being is the objective of the pure desire to know."[79] It is a known fact that human beings desire to know. Every moment of their existence is a moment of knowing.

We find that this desire to know is the dynamic force manifested in questions for intelligence and for reflection. It is not the verbal utterance of these questions; it is not the conceptual formulation of questions; it is not any insight or judgment. Rather, it is the drive that carries the cognitional process from merely

---

[78] Cronin *Foundations*, 86.
[79] *Insight*, 372.

perceiving to understanding, and from understanding to judging and to the complete context of correct judgments.[80] It is, in other words, simply the inquiring and critical spirit of the human person. This desire to know moves human beings to seek authentic understanding. This authentic understanding is necessitated by mechanism which inbuilt in *homosapiens* which Lonergan refers to as self-correcting process of learning. The desire to know moves people to seek the unconditioned, and prevents them from being contented with mere hearsay and unverified opinions.

This pure desire has an objective: it is the desire to know. As such, it desires not merely the satisfaction involved in knowing, but rather the contents of knowing. Both correct understanding and mistaken understanding (as long as not known to be mistaken) give satisfaction; but pure desire prizes the former and scorns the latter.

More precisely, the objective of the pure desire to know is "being", for it unfolds through the questions, "*what is it*"? and "*is it*"? These questions seek being; therefore being is the objective of the pure desire to know. The pure desire aims at, strives towards, intends "being". "Being" is all that is known, and all that remains to be known. Again, "being" is what is to be known through the totality of true judgments. Our definition is a second-order definition. Other definitions say what is meant. Ours tells us, not what is meant by "being", but how that meaning is to be determined.

The desire to know is called "pure" because it is not like other desires. It is to be known, not by comparing it to other desires, but simply by giving free rein to intelligent and rational consciousness. It is impalpable, but also powerful, for it pulls us out of the routine of perception and willing and of habit: it engages us in the search for solutions, makes us aloof to the unestablished, and compels assent to the unconditioned.[81] We shall now discuss how we reach the *virtually unconditioned*.

---

[80] *Insight*, 372.
[81] *Insight*, 373.

The Virtually Unconditioned

So far, what we have been accomplishing is asking and answering the first part of the *cognitional theoretic* question – What are we doing when we think we are knowing? – so that we can respond to the epistemological question – Why is doing that (namely, what we have verified that we actually do in knowing). Thus far, we have focused on what we were doing when our desire to understand supervened on our sensation, perception, or imaginations and wondering, asked the question for understanding questions such as What? Why? How? question. Now we need to reflect on and attend to the content of these activities as we move from mere thinking to knowing.

Every day we are compelled to make judgments. Our minds are dynamic and so, once we have understood and formulated the answer to our questions for understanding, we realize that our formulation is only *possibly* true or correct. When that realization occurs to us, we ask, "Is it so? Then we have reached the point of needing to make a judgment to answer that question. In order to do this, we need to attain a reflective insight. What is the process of answering questions for reflection in order to make sure our judgment is correct? Lonergan reminds us that first we have to perform an act of reflective understanding the aim of which is to ascertain whether the evidence for our judgment need is sufficient for the judgment to be true (or probable, or no more than possible depending on the degree of the evidence). It might require a prolonged effort of introspective analysis,[82] if we are going to grasp what we are actually doing when we make an evidence-based judgment, because we have first to gather all the evidence that is pertinent to the issue. Some evidence can easily be ascertained, for example, to questions such as "Is it raining now?" or "Is the English teacher coming to class today?" We don't need to take much time to answer "yes" or "no" to such reflective questions. On the other hand, questions such as, "Is the density of deposit in solution A the same as that of the mercury in solution B?" Answering immediately "yes" or "no" to such questions

---

[82] *Insight*, 304.

before taking the time to check would be rash. Now let us look at the general form of a reflective understanding.

Lonergan puts it that have we to grasp the sufficiency of evidence when reflecting about any prospective judgment in order to be able to posit the prospective judgment as true. All our judgments are contingent. This means that their occurrence or existence depends on the fulfillment of prior conditions. If the evidence shows that the required conditions have actually been fulfilled, then we have attained what he calls "the virtually unconditioned."[83] It is called *virtually* unconditioned because this is the case for everything but God: only God is *absolutely* to *formally* unconditioned, because God has no conditions whatsoever. The virtually unconditioned has conditions they are fulfilled *as a matter of fact*. Accordingly, a virtually unconditioned involves three elements, namely, (i) a conditioned, (2) a link between the conditioned and its conditions, and (3) the fulfilment of the conditions. We can express the above three elements in the *modus ponens* form of the syllogism: If A, then B. But A. Therefore B.

If James is reading this book, then his eyes are functioning (the link)

But James is reading this book (fulfillment)

Therefore, James' eyes are functioning (the fact of the conditioned)

The three elements of the above virtually unconditioned judgement are clear. The 'conditioned' is the judgement that "James' eyes are functioning". Its conditions are known (that if he is reading this book, then his eyes are functioning) and these conditions happened to be fulfilled in the sense that James "is reading this book". The question for reflection here is, "are the eyes of James functioning?" This question stands in need of evidence sufficient (that James is reading this book) for reasonable affirmation.

The function of reflective understanding is to meet the question for reflection by transforming the prospective judgment from the status of a conditioned to the status of a virtually unconditioned; and reflective understanding effects this transformation by grasping the

---

[83] *Insight*, 305.

conditions of the conditioned and their fulfilment.[84] A conditioned will be true only if all the conditions are fulfilled.

Correctness of Insights into Concrete Situation[85]

Now, one may ask, how do we distinguish between mere bright ideas and correct ones? Lonergan observes that insights, not only arise in answer to questions, but that they are also followed by further questions. Such further questions are of two kinds. They may stick to the initial issue or they may go on to raise distinct issues. The transition to other issues may happen for very different reasons. It may be because different interests intervene to draw attention elsewhere; the issue at hand may be not interesting, a person may tire of focusing on the same issue; the issue at hand may be difficult to comprehend. But, it may also be because the initial issue is exhausted, and therefore there are no further relevant questions to be asked.

We may conclude that insights are vulnerable when there are further questions to be asked on the same issue. But, when there are no further questions, the insight is invulnerable. Now in each one of us, there is a law which is immanent and operative in our cognitional processes. When an insight meets the issue squarely, when it hits the bull's eye, when it settles the matter, then there are no further relevant questions to ask, and so there are no further insights to challenge the initial position.[86] Therefore, at this point we can say that the insight is correct.

It is important to note that, it is not enough to say there are no further relevant questions "to me". "To me": this may suggest it is subjective to my whims and desires, but we need to lay a solid foundation on which the objective world may stand. There should be *in fact* no relevant questions whatsoever. But how is one to strike a happy balance between rashness and indecision? There is no short cut. However, Lonergan outlines some important factors[87] to be kept

---

[84] *Insight*, 305.
[85] This part is a paraphrase of *Insight*, 308-12.
[86] *Insight*, 309.
[87] *Insight*, 308-12.

in mind. First, one needs to give further questions a chance to arise. Secondly, one has to pose questions correctly. Thirdly, one has to be aware of the self-correcting process of learning. Finally, one needs to keep watch on one's temperament. We shall now explain in more detail the above four factors.

1. *Give further questions a chance to arise.* This involves intellectual alertness. We need to take time to discuss the issue at hand. Involving experts on the issue is of paramount importance. We too need to give room for possible related questions to emerge. We need to prevent biases from interfering with the discussion. Openness to further questions to arise is a characteristic of pure desire to know. We block further questions from arising when we are not willing to change our already established horizons.

2. *See that the problem is posed correctly.* It is very important that the question or problem is posed correctly. If we dodge this requirement we limit ourselves to a concrete situation diverging from expectations. To present a problem correctly, we need familiarity with the situation. But this means that, to make a correct judgment, we must already possess a large number of other correct judgments. But this is a vicious circle!

3. *The process of learning.* The vicious circle is broken by the process of learning. We acquire the required set of prior judgments not by judging them to be correct, but by taking over the judgments of others. This is called "learning", and it involves the suspension of personal judgment until such time as one is capable of verifying the borrowed judgments on one's own. The process of learning is a self-correcting process: the shortcomings of each insight provoke further questions and further insights.

4. *Temperament.* Rashness and indecision are based in temperament. The only thing to be done is to become aware of our temperament and to make a special effort to overcome our tendencies. Some people tend to rash so quickly to make judgements. Others may take too long to pass a judgment. It is only when all these factors are carefully observed a correct judgment is most likely to follow.

There is a philosophic theory that no one can ever be certain - skepticism. However, our purpose is to explain the facts. Human judgments oscillate about a mean. There are many points where even the rash person would not make a judgement, and there are many others where even the indecisive individual would not doubt. What then is the general form of such certitude of knowledge and ignorance? Our answer is in terms of the virtually unconditioned. There occurs a reflective insight in which at once one grasps: (1) a conditioned, that a given insight is correct; (2) a link between the conditioned and its conditions: a given insight is correct if it is invulnerable; and it is invulnerable if there are no further questions; (3) fulfillment: that the insight does put an end to further questions, and that this occurs in a mind that is alert, familiar with the situation, and master of it.

Self-Affirmation of the Knower[88]

We have discussed what judgment is. We have deliberated on the process to arrive at a correct judgment by an act of reflective understanding. Now the crucial question is whether correct judgments occur at all. The answer to this question is the act of making one. The most obvious and accurate judgment we can make now is that of self-affirmation - "I am a knower." This is a judgment of fact.

Let us analyze my judgment whether it is a virtually unconditioned. The conditioned here is the statement 'I am a knower.' The link between the conditioned and its conditions is the proposition 'I am a knower, if I am a concrete and intelligible unity-identity-whole, characterized by acts of sensing, perceiving, imagining, inquiring, understanding, formulating, reflecting, grasping the unconditioned, and judging.' The fulfilment of the conditions is given in consciousness.[89] There is no difficult in understanding the conditioned since we are expressing what is to be affirmed. The link also offers no difficulty since the conditions which it lists are familiar in our investigation. The difficult element lies in

---

[88] See *Insight* chapter 11 on Self-affirmation of the knower.
[89] *Insight*, 343-44.

the fulfilment of the conditions. The fulfilment is in the consciousness and we need now to familiarize ourselves with the various types of consciousness. We have empirical consciousness, intelligent consciousness and rational consciousness. These correspond with the three levels of inquiry.

The Notion of Consciousness

Consciousness is not an inward look. It is an awareness immanent in cognitional acts.[90] Lonergan explains what this "awareness" means. He says, "seeing is not merely a response to the stimulus of color and shape; it is a response that consists in becoming aware of color and shape. Hearing is not merely a response to the stimulus of sound; it is a response that consists in becoming aware of sound. As color differs from sound, so seeing differs from hearing. Still, seeing and hearing have a common feature, for in both occurrences there is not merely content but also conscious act."[91]

Three levels of Consciousness

The empirical consciousness is characterized by acts of sensing, perceiving, imagining. It correspond to the first level of inquiry, the level of data. The awareness immanent in these acts is the mere givenness of the acts. The intelligent consciousness is characterized by acts of inquiry, insight, and formulation. It corresponds to the second level of inquiry, the level of understanding. The rational consciousness is characterized by the grasp of the conditioned. It corresponds to the third level of inquiry, the level of judgement.

The Unity of Consciousness

The contents of consciousness cumulate into unities: what is experienced is what is understood; what is understood is what is affirmed. Similarly conscious acts also cumulate into unities. Many

---

[90] *Insight*, 344.
[91] *Insight*, 345.

acts coalesce into a single knowing. In fact, consciousness is much more of this unity than of separate acts. If there were no unity of consciousness, there would be no unity of contents. If there were no 'I', how could there be 'my experience' in which my inquiry occurred, and 'my reflection' and 'my judgment'?

Self-affirmation

After the preliminary clarifications, we return to our question, Am I a knower?

What do I mean by 'I'? The answer is difficult to formulate, but in some way I know very well what it means: it is neither the multiplicity nor the diversity of contents and conscious acts, but rather the unity that goes along with them. Do I discover a concrete and intelligible unity, identity, whole in my consciousness? If yes, then consciousness supplies the fulfillment of one element in the conditions for affirming that I am a knower.[92]

Does consciousness supply the fulfillment of the other conditions too? Here each one must ask himself or herself: have I had experiences of sensing, perceiving, imagining, inquiry, understanding, formulating, reflecting, grasping evidence as sufficient, judging? In the very process of the asking and the answering, one will discover these experiences.

If then I can discover both a concrete and intelligible unity in the data of my consciousness, and if this unity is characterized by acts on the three levels of experiencing, understanding, and judging, then I can make the judgment, I am a knower. This is the judgment of self-affirmation.

To answer negatively is to contradict myself. To answer 'No' to the question is incoherent. The answer 'I don't know' is also incoherent. The only option is the silence of the vegetable: if I really knew noting, I could not explain my ignorance. The talking skeptic is involved in a contradiction. This contradiction is not a logical contradiction: it is not a contradiction in what he is saying. It is an

---

[92] *Insight*, 352.

exercised contradiction, between what he is saying and what he is doing.

Further: naturally and spontaneously the activities occur within me. Cognitional process does not lie outside the realm of natural law. With statistical regularity, the acts of knowing occur. Spontaneously the question for intelligence arises. Spontaneously the question for reflection arises; it demands the absolute and refuses unreserved assent to anything less than the virtually unconditioned.

I can control what I sense and imagine; but I cannot escape sensations and images altogether. I can ridicule intelligence and reduce its use to a minimum; but I cannot eliminate it altogether. I can criticize everything, but not the critical spirit itself. Thus the deepest foundation of our knowing is pragmatic engagement in that process. Even to seek such a foundation involves a vicious circle: we have to employ our knowing in order to reach such foundations for knowing.

The Impossibility of Revision[93]

Is the self-affirmation that we have been engaged in, descriptive or explanatory? To answer this, we must point out that, while we began our study of insight descriptively and with examples, we moved on to explanation. Explanation means relating related things among themselves. Thus we defined data and the level of experience as what is presupposed by inquiry and insight; and our account of judgment and reflective understanding itself consisted in relating these to understanding and experience.

Thus there are two types of description and two types of explanation. One begins from the data of sense (e.g. empirical science) and the other from the data of consciousness (cognitional theory). The important difference between the two is that explanation on the basis of sense can reduce the element of hypothesis to a minimum, but it cannot eliminate it altogether, whereas explanation on the basis of consciousness can escape entirely the merely supposed. This does not mean that minor revisions are impossible.

---

[93] *Insight* 359-60.

What is excluded is the radical revision involving a shift in fundamental terms and relations. For what would such revision involve? It would have to appeal to data, present a better understanding of data, and affirm that this understanding was better, more correct. But this would amount to reaffirming the three levels of cognitional process.

The Notion of Objectivity[94]

Human knowing is complex: it is not any single activity, but a structured set of activities, in which we can distinguish three levels: presentations, intelligence, and reflection. It is also cumulative: single judgments cluster into the context named knowledge or mentality. This complexity in our knowing implies a parallel complexity in our notion of objectivity. Thus we distinguish: a principal notion of objectivity, which is contained within a patterned context of judgments which implicitly define the terms, object and subject; partial aspects of objectivity: an experiential aspect, proper to sense and empirical consciousness; a normative aspect, contained in the contrast between the detached and unrestricted desire to know on the one hand, and merely subjective desires and fears on the other; an absolute aspect, contained in single judgments, inasmuch as each rests on a grasp of the unconditioned.

The Principal Notion

The principal notion of objectivity is contained within a patterned context of judgments which implicitly define the terms, object and subject.

An *object* is any A, B, C, D, ..., where A, B, C, D, ... are defined by the correctness of the set of judgments. A *subject* is any object, say A, where it is true that A affirms himself or herself as a knower in the sense explained in the chapter on Self-affirmation.

---

[94] *Insight* 399-409. This is the summary of the notion of objectivity as given in Chapter 13 of *Insight*.

In a simpler way, if I can make a set of judgments in the pattern, "I am a knower," "This is a computer," and if I can add further, "I am not this computer," I reach the principal notion of objectivity.

Further, insofar as I can intelligently grasp and reasonably affirm the existence of other knowers besides myself, I can add to the list of objects that are also subjects.

Properties of the Principal Notion

1. The notion resides, not in any single judgment, but in a context of other judgments.

2. It is not contained in any experiential or normative factor occurring prior to judgment.

3. The validity of the notion is the same as the validity of the set of judgments that contain it, that is, if these judgments are correct, then it is true that there are objects and subjects in the sense defined.

4. The judgments in the appropriate pattern commonly are made and regarded as correct. Therefore commonly people will know objects and subjects, and commonly they will be surprised that there should be any doubt about this. However, it does not follow that they will be able to give an account of their knowledge of objects and subjects. They tend to jump to the conclusion that so evident a matter as the existence of objects and subjects must rest on something as obvious as the experiential aspect of objectivity. Hence they will say that the table is an object because they see it or feel it.

5. The principal notion is closely related to the notion of being. There is objectivity only if there are distinct beings, some of which both know themselves and know others as others. The subject himself has to be within being, because apart from being there is nothing. If she is within being, then she is either the whole of being or a part of it. If she is the whole of being, then the principal notion of objectivity will not arise. Only if she is a part, and there are other parts distinct from her, and she knows both herself and these parts as distinct from her, then the principal notion arises.

6. The principal notion solves the problem of transcendence [the critical problem in the standard formulation, or the problem of the

bridge]. This problem is usually framed as: How does the knower get beyond herself to a known? The question itself is misleading. It supposes the knower to know herself and asks how she knows anything else. Our answer is: (i) the knower may experience herself and think of herself, but she can know herself only in judgment. (ii) Other judgments are equally possible and reasonable. So there arises knowledge of other objects both as beings and as being distinct from the knower. Therefore transcendence does not consist in going beyond a known knower; rather, it is a heading for being within which there are differences, among them the difference between object and subject.

Absolute Objectivity

Absolute objectivity is one of the partial aspects of objectivity. Whereas the principal notion of objectivity is contained in a patterned set of judgments, absolute objectivity pertains to judgments as single. Its ground is the virtually unconditioned that is grasped by reflective understanding and posited in judgment.

Because the content of a judgment is an absolute, it is not relative to the subject uttering it, to the time and place of its utterance. For example, Nelson Mandela, the former president of South Africa, died in 2013: if this is true, then it is true always and at all times.

Note: to affirm that something is, does not imply that it is within space. If "X is" means "X is within space," then "space is" should mean "space is within space", and so on indefinitely. The same argument holds for being within time. "To be" cannot be always "to be at some time". So interpretations of being or of absolute objectivity in terms of space and time are mere intrusions of imagination. Absolute objectivity is simply a property of the unconditioned; and the unconditioned, as such, says nothing about space and time. "To be" does not necessarily mean "to be within space and time."

Normative Objectivity

Normative objectivity is objectivity as opposed to the subjectivity of wishful thinking, of rash judgments, of allowing emotions and feelings to interfere with the proper development of cognitional process. Its ground is in the unfolding of the unrestricted, detached, pure desire to know. Because it is unrestricted, it is opposed to hiding the truth, or blocking access to it. Because it is detached, it is opposed to the interference of other human desires and fears. To be objective in the normative sense is to give free rein to the pure desire to know, to questions for intelligence and for reflection. It involves distinguishing between questions that admit immediate solutions and questions that do not. It also means distinguishing between sound questions and meaningless or illegitimate ones.

Experiential Objectivity

Experiential objectivity is the given as given. It is the field of materials about which one inquires, and in which one finds fulfilment of conditions.

The given is unquestionable and indubitable: as it is not the answer to any question, it cannot be upset by further questions. It is given prior to questioning, and is unaffected by our questioning. So in itself, it is indubitable, it cannot be doubted.

This given is equally valid in all its parts, but differently significant. It is differently significant in the sense that some parts are significant for some departments of knowledge, and other parts for others. Thus, e.g., the physicist disregards dreams, but the psychoanalyst takes them as his subject matter.

Note: we are employing the name 'given' in an extremely broad sense. It includes not only sensations, but also images, dreams, illusions, hallucinations, subjective bias, etc. Why is this so? Because our account of the given is extrinsic. This means that we do not try to describe the given, or the stream of consciousness; we do not discuss how much the subject contributes to making up the given, nor how much 'outside' agents do. We only noted that reflection presupposes understanding, and that understanding presupposes something to be understood, materials for inquiry. Such materials we have been calling the 'given'. Such materials must be indubitable, and equally valid in all their parts. Were they all invalid, there could be neither inquiry nor reflection, and so no reasonable pronouncement that they are invalid. Were some valid and others invalid, there would have to be a principle of selection. But such a principle can be grasped only after inquiry has begun. Prior to inquiry there can be no discrimination and so no rejection.

Lonergan's Contribution

1. Lonergan leads us to identify the critical spirit in us. This is spirit to know and understand. This spirit is not found in other animals who cannot raise questions. It is the inner pure desire to know. This desire is completely different from other desires. Others desires may be seeking survival or other self-regarding interests. The pure desire to know is detached and disinterested, and seeks only to know what is to be known and to be understood correctly.

2. In other words, Lonergan leads us to identify our experience of knowing. He leads us to identify our experience of experiencing, to identify our experience of understanding, and to identify our experience of reaching judgment. In our moments of knowing do we identify these acts in our consciousness?

3. More specifically, Lonergan helps us to make a transition from mere thinking to correct knowing. This is simply a movement from cognitional structure to epistemology. We transit from the question, 'what are we doing when we think we are knowing?' to the question 'what is doing that knowing?'

4. Lonergan offers a unique method to reach objectivity. The principal notion of objectivity helps us to distinguish between object and subject (the traditional question of the bridge). Then he deepens our awareness of objectivity by clearly presenting the three partial aspects of objectivity – the experiential, the normative and the absolute aspects.

5. Lonergan has directed us on how to reach the question of doing. The same intelligent and rational consciousness grounds the doing as well as the knowing. It is a matter of moving from the third level to the fourth level of consciousness.

Concluding Remarks and Suggestions

1. Human knowing is an activity that as a matter of fact constitutes us as knowers, which occurs through a dynamic structure with three successive levels.

2. We have come to understand that knowing is not simply "taking a look" at things that exist outside the person. We have been made to realize that the cognitional structure is natural and inevitably at work in every knower, even though it is rarely formally recognized. The first level of experience provides the data that allows for the possibility of an insight to emerge. This second level is the moment of catching on, the moment of understanding. The third is the level of judgement, which follows and acts upon insight. It is only after reaching the unconditioned that we proceed to pass judgment. The three parts of the cognitional structure presuppose and complement each other.

3. What we have accomplished so far is to ask and answer the *cognitional theoretic* question – What are we doing when we think we are knowing? Only after successfully accomplishing that can we respond to the *epistemological* question – Why is doing in that (namely, what we have verified that we actually do in knowing). Instead of starting from the false presuppositions of conventional epistemology's question – How do we know that we know? – namely, the problem of the bridge between the subject *in here* and the object *out there* based on the unfounded supposition of there being a subject/object split. This formulation of the epistemological question arises because the cognitional theoretic question has either not been asked, or, if asked, incorrectly answered, usually because the questioner presumes that the subject is *in here* and the object is *already out there now reality* reached by just 'taking a look'.

4. The existential being does not know just for the sake of knowing. The existential decisions of the subject are what constitute his/her very being as a conscious, responsible human being. He/she raises the question of doing. How therefore do we do? In order to "do," one has to decide. There is a very close connection between the process of knowing and the process of deciding. Lonergan contends that the same intelligent and rational consciousness grounds the

doing as well as the knowing.[95] It is a matter of moving from the third level to the fourth level of self-consciousness.

5. We have also been lead to understand how we reach objectivity of our knowing. We follow the same process in reaching the objectivity of our doing.

6. We suggest the following three things:

    a. As true human knowers let's take time and understand the process of knowing which at times may be complex.
    b. Let's us appropriate the process of reaching genuine objectivity.
    c. Let's avoid inconsistency between knowing and doing.

The next chapter will introduce us to one of the most important principles in moral consistency - the Golden Rule.

Case Study 2: Reporting on the Death of Gerald

When the great musician took his life in July of 2011, major news organizations covered the story in great detail. Some media houses revealed graphic details about the method Gerald had used. While there was great interest on the part of the public in finding out what had happened, many argued that reporting too much detail about the suicide violated the family's privacy.

Indeed, many of Gerald's fans posted comments on Facebook, Twitter, and other social networks expressing their objections to the media treatment of the suicide and urging reporters to respect the family's right to grieve in peace. Several members of the medical health profession specializing in mental health also took issue with the detailed reports.

This was a statement from the Free Press Commission, "When reporting suicide, care should be taken to avoid excessive detail about the method used." Yet some journalists argued that the primary responsibility of the media was to report the story truthfully and factually.

---

[95] *Insight*, 622.

One of the top independent journalists wrote, "Journalists should report it as long as it remains of interest to the public. It is not a journalist's job to protect us from the ugly facts. The journalist's duty is not to do good or be wise, but to report the whole story, which may in fact be a part of a larger story unfolding elsewhere."

Questions for Discussion

1. Looking at the whole incident, identify the main problem.
2. In the above case, who can be termed "responsible", the journalist/reporter or those who spread the news on the social media?
3. Would the journalists have harmed the public by not reporting the "whole truth?" In other words, were they ethically required to report all the details?
4. Can differentiate between the judgment of fact (factual truth) and the judgment of value (moral truth) in this case?

III. The Golden Rule

But there are stages in human development when there is no probability that men will apprehend and consent to a universally accessible and permanent solution that meets the basic problem of human nature. Moreover, all human development has been seen to be compounded with decline, and so it fails to prepare men directly and positively to apprehend and consent to the solution.[96]

Questions for Reflection

1. Do you feel that you should treat others as you want to be treated yourself?
2. Do you treat others fairly?
3. How do you feel when others treat you badly?
4. Have you ever tried to "step into another's shoes?"

Introduction

The Golden Rule (GR) is one the most popular moral principles in the history of humankind. It is generally viewed as the principle of harmony or fair treatment. It is believed that the earliest affirmation of the maxim of reciprocity, reflecting the ancient Egyptian goddess Ma'at, appears in the story of "The Eloquent Peasant", which dates to the Middle Kingdom (c. 2040 -1650 BCE). And it was expressed in this way: "Now this is the command: Do to the doer to make him do."[97] The oldest platinum rule is from Hinduism which states "One should always treat others as they wish to be treated" (*Hitopadehsa*,

---

[96] *Insight*, 720.

[97] John Albert Wilson, *The Culture of Ancient Egypt*, (Chicago: University of Chicago Press, 1956) 121.

from before 2000 BCE). The term "Golden Rule" or "Golden Law" traces its genesis back to the early 17th century in Britain and its use by Anglican theologians and preachers. The earliest known usage is that by the Anglicans Charles Gibbon and Thomas Jackson in 1604.[98] This maxim is found in all world religions and cultures, with little variations from one religion (or culture) to another. Let us now see various formulations of the rule.

The Golden Rule in the Twelve Religions of the World

1. Bahá'í Faith: Ascribe not to any soul that which thou wouldst not have ascribed to thee, and say not that which thou does not. - *Baha'u'llah.*

2. Brahmanism: This is the sum of Dharma [duty]: Do naught unto others which would cause you pain if done to you. - *Mahabharata, 5:1517*

3. Buddhism: Hurt not others in ways that you yourself would find hurtful. *Udana-Varga 5:18*

4. Christianity: So whatever you wish that men would do to you, do so to them; for this is the Law and the Prophets. *Matthew 7:12 RSV.*

5. Confucianism: What I do not wish men to do to me, I also wish not to do to men. *Analects 15:23*

6. Hinduism: This is the sum of duty: do not do to others what would cause pain if done to you. *Mahabharata 5:1517*

7. Islam: None of you [truly] believes until he wishes for his brother what he wishes for himself. *Number 13 of Imam Al-Nawawi's Forty Hadiths.*

8. Jainism: A man should wander about treating all creatures as he himself would be treated. *Sutrakritanga 1.11.33*

---

[98] Antony Flew, *ed.* "Golden Rule" in *A Dictionary of Philosophy* (London: The MacMillan Press, 1979) 125.

9. Judaism: What is hateful to you, do not to your fellow man. This is the law: all the rest is commentary. *Talmud, Shabbat 31a.*

10. Sikhism: As thou deemest thyself so deem others. Then shalt thou become a partner in heaven. *Kabir*

11. Taoism: Regard your neighbor's gain as your own gain; and regard your neighbor's loss as your own loss. *T'ai Shang kan ying P'ien.*

12. Zoroastrianism: That nature only is good when it shall not do unto another whatever is not good for its own self. *Didastan-i-dinik*

All the formulations above have something in common. They all seem to agree that doing good to others should be the basis of all human behavior and relationships. They are summaries of a social justice that needs to be propagated universally.

Seven Variations (or Relatives) of the Golden Rule

a. Golden Rule: Do unto others as you would have them do unto you. Also known as *law of reciprocity.*

b. Silver Rule: Do not do unto others as you would not want done to you. Also known as the *negative formulation* of the Golden Rule.

c. Platinum Rule: Treat others the way they want to be treated.

d. The Rule of Love: Love others as you do yourself (or even better than yourself).

e. Role Taking: Put yourself in others' shoes in order to know how to treat them ethically.

f. Empathy: Feel and care about the suffering of others.

g. Kant's Categorical Imperative: Act only according to that maxim whereby you can, at the same time, will that it should become a universal law.

Socrates and the Golden Rule

Socrates is reported by Plato in his *Crito* to have said that one must never do harm to another. He also said that one must never return evil to anyone. In the *Republic* we read a similar sentiment expressed by Socrates. He argues that it is never just to injure any man and that the doctrine [practice??] of retaliation for injuries could not have been initiated by any of the wise men but must have been devised by some famous tyrant such as Periander, Perdiccas, or Xerxes. The entire argument of the Gorgias revolves around the proposition that one cannot injure another without injury to oneself. Plato presents Socrates' morality as one that embraces both friends and enemies.

After Socrates was condemned to death by the men of Athens, he was asked to choose the punishment that he deserved. He surprised the jury by proposing that he be given a meal in the Prytaneum (this was a stadium where Olympic champions were treated with great respect and honour after their victory). But the Athenian elders remained determined to kill him. Socrates then gave this final speech: "You men, who have condemned me to death, should know that *vengeance will come upon you* right after my death, inflicted by Zeus and much more painful than the vengeance you will inflict by killing me. For you have now done this deed supposing that you will be released from giving an account of your life, but it will *turn out much the opposite for you*, as I affirm. There will be more who will refute you, whom I have now been holding back; you did not perceive them. And *they will be harsher,* inasmuch as they are younger, and you will be more indignant. For if you suppose that by killing human beings you will prevent someone from reproaching you for not living correctly, you do not think nobly."[99]

This speech contains suggestions of the Golden Rule. It is as if Socrates was telling the jury to "do unto me what you wish to be done unto you."

---

[99] *Plato's Apology of Socrates,* 39c. Italics are mine, to emphasize the GR.

Golden Rule and Role-Taking

The Golden Rule enjoys widespread but not universal assent. It demands that before acting, a person should ask him/herself, "If I were in the place of the other, would I like to be treated in the same way?" This indicates to me that I should avoid acting according to rules to which I might later object when someone acts on them in dealing with me. Nevertheless, I may be led to think that there is no likelihood of my ever being in the same position myself. Let us take an example. Suppose I am a forty-year-old male doctor and confronted with a case of assisting a 16-year-old girl to procure an abortion. I know clearly that this situation will never happen to me. In this case, it is obviously awkward to ask the literal question, "What if I were to find myself in her predicament?"

The Golden Rule demands we go beyond the literal meaning of the question. It demands that we have an imaginative mind. (We shall see this aspect in Gensler's analysis later). We need to imagine being in the other person's position even though we may never be in it. We need to go beyond our actual space and time. There are many situations which we have not yet experienced and which we may never actually experience in life. Taken in this sense, the Golden Rule gives us the possibility of going even beyond the world of human beings. Let us suppose we see a cat stuck in a well struggling to get out. Can we use the principle of the Golden Rule to rescue this cat? For sure, we will never experience life as a cat, and so it is pointless to ask ourselves, "What if I were in the position of this cat?" But, with our new understanding, it is possible to go beyond the "literal cat" and imagine the situation at hand.

Kant's Objection of the Golden Rule

The categorical imperative of Immanuel Kant is the central philosophical concept in his deontological moral reasoning. It is found in his 1785 groundbreaking book, *Groundwork of the Metaphysics of Morals*. His first formulation of the categorical imperative reads thus, "Act only in accordance with that maxim through which you can at the same time will that it become a universal law".[100] It is sometimes knowns as "the principle of universalization".

According to Kant, the GR is inferior to this imperative. He claims that the GR does not contain principles of duties to one's own will. Secondly, the GR does not contain principles of strict obligation to one another.[101] Hence, the GR could not be a universal law.

Kant's objection to the GR as being inferior to the categorical imperative is suspect. This is because his formulation sounds very similar to the GR, and it seems likely that it traces its roots back to the GR itself. It even sounds like a paraphrase of the GR. The main difference in the formulation of the two principles is that while the categorical imperative contains the words "universal law" explicitly, the GR does not (though the term "universal law" is implied).

The first major criticism of Kant's reasoning came from the French philosopher Benjamin Constant, who claimed that if truth telling must be universal, then following Kant's categorical imperative, one should tell a known murderer the location of his intended victim. Since Kant was still alive at the time, he responded to Constant. He agreed with Constant's inference (that one has a moral duty not to lie to a murderer). However, Kant argued that for philanthropic concerns, one should not reveal the truth to the murderer. One can also refuse to answer murderer's question. However, Kant denied that such an inference indicates any weakness in his premises. Kant's objections to the GR were also challenged by Gensler as described below.

The Golden Rule Promotes Good, not Evil

The Golden Rule states "do unto others as you would have them do unto you." This maxim, if taken literally, can have unexpected repercussions. The meaning of the Rule can be twisted in such a way that it can become legitimate to steal, to lie, to seduce,

---

[100] Sally Sedgwick, *Kant's Groundwork of the Metaphysics of Morals: An Introduction*, (Cambridge: Cambridge University Press, 2008) 108. Cited hereafter as Sedgwick *Groundwork*.

[101] Sedgwick, *Groundwork*, 140.

to insult, to kidnap, to inflict pain or even to kill, if I'm willing for the other to do the same to me. It is as simple as that. Suppose I am a sadist, and I find joy in inflicting pain on others, and I'm also willing to receive the same treatment myself, then I can easily justify my actions with reference to the Golden Rule. Suppose I live in an environment in which warfare is a daily occurrence, and I have been made to believe that war is a legitimate way of life, then I can easily justify my willingness to kill using the Golden Rule maxim. Taken this way, the Golden Rule can be used to justify any form of evil so long as the perpetrator is himself ready to receive the same treatment.

However, what we should not forget here is that the Golden Rule is an ethical maxim. It is not designed to approve any kind of vice. It is meant to be a means of achieving virtue. The Golden Rule is a device encouraging us to do to others what ought to be done to them. It is a means for counteracting a natural tendency to ignore peoples' rights and needs. As Paul Weiss[102] observes, this maxim can have this good effect only (a) if we know what we want, (b) if what we want is identical with what we ought to desire, and (c) if what is [in fact] good for us is also good for the rest. According to Weiss, the Golden Rule promotes good rather than evil only when all the three conditions happen to be fulfilled. The Golden Rule seeks the good of the other.

The Golden Rule and Altruism

Let us reflect on the phrase 'do to others.' This phrase is a recognition of the fact that human beings have an inbuilt power to make a deliberate choice to reach out to the other. This is altruism. Altruism is the capacity to make a transition from our own comfort zone to the unfamiliar (or less familiar) grounds of others. It is that inherent desire which moves us to moral action. It is that pure desire which enables us to look the other in the eye with love and compassion. This is a call for self-appropriation which we discussed in chapter one. The Golden Rule assumes that the agent has an adequate knowledge of him/herself. This is because he/she needs first

---

[102] Paul Weiss, "The Golden Rule" in *Journal of Philosophy*, Vol. 38, No. 16 (Jul. 31, 1941), 421-430. Cited hereafter as Weiss, "The Golden Rule".

to know him/herself so that he/she can now, to some extent compare him/herself with the other (after understanding that human beings have more things in common than differences). He/she is supposed to have some knowledge of his/her own needs so that he/she can imagine the needs of the other and be moved to action.

In a highly individualistic society, this maxim tends to change its meaning to "do for yourself what you would have others do for you." This sounds true for those who consider themselves highly self-sufficient. It seems to suggest that they don't need others in their existence. In addition, if anything good is done to them, they may reject or become indifferent to it. Similarly, people may use the same maxim when they are neglected by the society. The Golden Rule urges us to treat others as end in themselves thus embracing the categorical imperative of Kant: "Never treat yourself or another rational being merely as a means, but in every case, at the same time, treat him as an end in itself as well."

Gensler's Formulation of the Golden Rule[103]

Harry J. Gensler's formulation of the Golden Rule solves the problem raised by its critics such as Kant. His formulation reads, **"Treat others only as you consent to being treated in the same situation."** According to Gensler, the GR forbids the combination of two things: [1] I do something to another, and [2] I'm unwilling that this be done to me in the same situation. From the two statements, it is clear that the Golden Rule requires that we treat others only as we consent to be being treated in the same situation. In its application, the GR requires consistency, knowledge and imagination. We shall see the importance of these three elements for the GR to be used effectively as a moral principle.

---

[103] Harry J. Gensler, *Ethics: A Contemporary Introduction*, (London: Routledge Publishers, 2011) 81-96. I have taken the whole of this section from Gensler's book. Some parts of this section are identical with the book, while few parts are my own imagination.

The Application of the GR Theorem

To apply the GR, you imagine yourself in the other person's place, at the receiving end of the action. If you act in a given way toward another and yet are unwilling to be treated that way yourself in the same situation, then you violate the Rule. Let us take an example. Suppose an employer dismisses an employee from his firm. Before we can judge whether the employee was dismissed fairly or unfairly, we need to get the reasons for the dismissal (gathering knowledge). Then, after getting enough information, we put ourselves in the place of the dismissed employee (imagination). And then, we ask ourselves, "Am I now willing for this to be done to me in the same situation (consistency)?" When combined with knowledge and imagination, the GR is a powerful tool of moral thinking. Though the GR is a consistency principle, it does not replace regular moral norms. It is not an infallible guide on what is right or wrong. It only prescribes consistency, namely, that our actions (toward another) be in harmony with our desires (about a reversed-situation action).

The Literal Golden Rule (LR)

We have to be careful with the literal formulation of the Golden Rule. This is formulated as "Treat others as you want to be treated." If you want P to do something to you, then do this same thing to P. It has no "same-situation" clause. In many cases it works well. Suppose you want to be loved by Jane, then love Jane. If you don't want to be injured in a game, then don't injure others. This application sounds perfect. But in some instances, this application may lead to absurdities in two different ways: first, you may be in a different situation from P, and secondly, you may have defective desires about how you are to be treated. Let us take some examples:

1. To a patient: if you want a doctor to remove your appendix, then you should remove the doctor's appendix.

2. To a violent little boy who loves to fight: if you want your sister to fight you, then fight with her.

3. To a parent: if you want your child not to punish you, then don't punish him.

4. To one who desires to be hated (defective desires): if you want others to hate you, then hate them.

The LR leads to absurdities because it does not have the "same-situation" clause. It ignores differences in situations.

In applying the GR, we need to ask, "Am I now willing that if I were in the same situation then this be done to me (first question)?" There is something important we need to note in the GR. The Golden Rule is about our present reaction to a hypothetical case. We need to ask, "Am I now willing that if I were in the same situation, then this be done to me?" The question should not be, "If I were in the same situation, would I then be willing that this be done to me (2nd Question)?" The difference is subtle but important.

Gensler gives a very interesting example to help us understand this subtle hypothetical difference. Suppose I have a two-year-old son, little Willy, who keeps putting his fingers into electrical outlets. I try to discourage him from doing this, but nothing works. Finally, I decide that I need to spank him when he does it again. I want to see if I can spank him without violating the GR. In determining this, I should ask the first question, not the second: Am I now willing that if I were in Willy's place in the same situation then I should be spanked? If I were in Willy's place in the reversed situation, would I then be willing to be spanked? This has "willing that if." It's about my present adult desire toward a hypothetical case. This has "if" before "willing." It's about the desire I'd have as a small child.

With the first question, I imagine myself this way: I'm a two-year-old child. I put my fingers into electrical outlets, and the only thing that will stop me is a spanking. As a two-year old, I don't understand electricity and so I desire not to be spanked. As an adult, I say "I *now* desire that if I were in this situation then I be spanked." I might add, "I'm thankful that my parents spanked me in such cases, even though I wasn't pleased then." Thus, I can spank my child without breaking the GR, since I'm willing that I would have been treated in the same way in the same situation. On the other hand, if I were in Willy's place and thus judged things from a two-year-old mentality, then I would desire not to be spanked. That's what the crossed-out question is about. If we formulated the GR using this, then I'd break the GR if I spanked Willy. But this is absurd. We need to formulate the GR correctly, in terms of my present reaction to a hypothetical case. I can satisfy the demands of GR because I'm now (as an adult) willing that I would have been spanked in this situation. This point is subtle but of central importance.

This distinction is crucial when we deal with someone who is not very rational, such as the person who is drunk, senile or in a vegetative situation. Properly understood, the GR is about our *present* attitude toward a hypothetical case. To use the GR correctly, I should say "I am willing that if"; I shouldn't say "I *would* be willing." The GR does not tell us what specific action to take. Instead, it forbids inconsistent combinations.

Our GR formulation has three key features:

a. a *same-situation* clause,

b. a *present attitude* toward a hypothetical situation, and

c. a *don't-combine* form.

These features are extremely important to avoid absurd implications such as those found in Kant's objection to the GR. Kant does not consider the above three features and especially a same-situation clause. He only takes the literal meaning of the Rule. Kant also ignores a *present attitude* toward a hypothetical situation.

Golden Rule Fallacies[104]

Gensler lists six possible fallacies, which could arise from improper understanding of Golden Rule. I will briefly summarize them.

1. The *literal GR fallacy* assumes that everyone has the same likes, dislikes, and needs that we have. So, we treat others *in their situation* exactly as we want them to treat us *in our situation*. However, this is not the case. On the contrary, we often need to grasp another's uniqueness, and imagine ourselves being in his/her shoes (which includes their likes and dislikes), and then ask: "Am I now

---

[104] Harry J. Gensler, *Ethics and the Golden Rule*, (London: Routledge Publishers, 2013) 28.

of insights, to the level of making true judgments. The subject progresses to making meaningful deliberations. It is this process of self-appropriation that helps a person to make right decision for him/herself and for the others.

The method of self-appropriation challenges a person to embrace the normativity of the transcendental precepts, that is, to be attentive, to be intelligent, to be reasonable and to be responsible.[107] The Golden Rule is implied in these transcendental precepts. How does a person know what to do "unto others" if he/she is not attentive enough to their own needs and likes? How do they know how to attend to others if they have not delved into understanding their world? How does a person reach out to others if he/she is not reasonable in his/her judgements? And finally, how can we expect someone to make altruistic decisions if he/she is not ready to be responsible? This is the richness and the beauty of Lonergan's transcendental method.

Lonergan's Contribution

Lonergan's transcendental method directs us to embrace the golden rule in a more authentic and humane manner. His transcendental precepts which challenges us to be attentive to others' needs, to be intelligent in understanding the ecosystem (which comprises human beings, animals, and other living and non-living things) in which live, to be reasonable in the judgements we pass after understanding the social milieu and to take responsibility in our rational decisions and actions to others.

Concluding Remarks and Suggestions

1. Golden rule is an ethical maxim which has met with tremendous universal commendation. It is a key component in moral integrity.

2. Gensler has shown the two different senses in which we can view the Rule – the literal and the true, meaningful sense. The Golden

---

[107] *Method*, 20.

Rule is often mistakenly interpreted in the literal sense which can be very misleading. The new formulation of the Golden Rule is "Treat others only as you consent to being treated in the same situation."

3. We suggest the following:
   a. We should clearly differentiate between the Golden Rule and the Literal Rule.
   b. In application of the Golden Rule, we should never forget the "same situation" clause.
   c. We too, should not forget to apply 'a *present attitude* toward a hypothetical situation.'
   d. We should, by all means, avoid Golden Rule fallacies.

Having examined one of the greatest principles of moral reasoning, we shall go ahead to explore another "inner principle", perhaps the principle which controls the other principles – the moral conscience.

Case Study 3: "Mercy Killing"

Mr. Johnson has been admitted to a high profile hospital in the city. He has been in a vegetative state for the last 6 months, and the doctors are saying that there is no sign that he will improve. He is suffering from lung cancer. The doctors are doing their best, but the situation is becoming worse. He is in great pain. He has pleaded with the doctors to let him "die with dignity", that is, to inject him with lethal chlorophyll. The doctors are reluctant to administer this injection (because of their Hippocratic Oath). The parents of Johnson are able to pay hospital bills and at the same time they are distressed at seeing the terrible suffering of their son.

Questions for Deliberation

1. Consider yourself in place of Johnson. The Golden Rule states that you treat others as you would like to be treated in a similar situation. Would you not like to be relieved of such pain if you were in the same position as Johnson?
2. Are the doctors justified in their refusal to administer the injection?
3. Are the doctors violating the Golden Rule principle?

4. Should the parents of Johnson allow the doctors to administer a lethal injection?
5. If the doctors administer the injection, will they be morally consistent with their professional responsibilities?

IV. The Notion of Conscience

It is by the transcendental notion of value and its expression in a good and an uneasy conscience that man can develop morally. But a rounded moral judgment is ever the work of a fully developed self-transcending subject or, as Aristotle would put it, of a virtuous man.[108]

Questions for Reflection

1. What do you understand by conscience?
2. What are the different types of consciences?
3. Can we have a correct or right conscience?
4. Can we have a "collective conscience"?
5. Can the community be the "conscience" of its people?

Introduction

There is no doubt that authority and truth are in crisis in contemporary society. Conscience, too, is in a precarious state. This is, perhaps, because of the increasing level of relativism in all spheres of life. Contemporary man/woman is skeptical about authority and the existence of "the real" or any sort of objective truth. He/she is doubtful about the possibility of reaching a consensus about moral issues – the value of his/her moral actions.

Yet there is one thing which remain constant in the lives of human beings and which make them superior to other species. They are the only beings that can make rational choices. To some extent, these choices need some standard by which to measure their worth

---

[108] *Method*, 41.

and direction. Having rejected the standard of authority and that of objective truth, the only choice remaining is conscience. Now, what is the foundation of the human conscience if we have rejected external authority and objective truth? This brings us to the awkward question of our conscience. Without any solid foundation for our conscience, how can it really be trusted? Can my conscience err? If I am in error, what is the point of reference? These questions point to the fact that we cannot rely solely on our own conscience to make rational choices. We need some external assistance. In this chapter we shall discuss some of the elements that are vital in the formation of conscience. Before we do that, let us try to clarify the meaning of the word "conscience".

The Etymology of the Word "Conscience"

The word "conscience" comes from Latin word *conscire* in which the prefix *con* means "with" while the suffix *scire* means "to know". The suffix is also related to the Latin word *scientia* which means "science", "knowledge", "awareness" or "acquaintance." Putting the two parts together, we are led to deduce that the term "conscience" simply means "with knowledge." Thus, in our decision making, we are expected to act "with knowledge." As we seek to acquire a better understanding of the term "conscience", let us keep its etymological meaning in mind.

Conscience is not an "inner voice" telling a person what to do and what to avoid. Conscience in the strictest sense can be defined as a faculty (in the intellect) of moral judgment that distinguishes between right and wrong. Conscience is closely related to another Greek term, *synderesis*.

Synderesis

Synderesis or *synteresis*, is a Greek word used in scholastic moral philosophy, to describe the natural capacity or disposition (habitus) of the practical reason to apprehend intuitively the universal first principles of human action.[109] It is the innate principle in the moral consciousness of every person that directs the agent to good and restrains him from doing evil. This implies that in every human, there is an innate principle which in one way or another directs his or her actions. This principle is very important in decision making and cannot be simply wished away. The scholastic thinkers called it the spark from which the light of conscience arises. This 'spark' lights a fire in the conscience and the person is motivated to do the right thing. *Synderesis* is also considered as the capacity to apprehend the first principles of metaphysics such as the principle of non-contradiction. Having understood the meaning of *synderesis*, let us look into different types of consciences.

Seven Types of Consciences

In this section, I present seven types of consciences, namely, correct, erroneous, certain doubtful, lax, scrupulous and delicate consciences.

1. Delicate Conscience: People with a delicate conscience take a substantial amount of time to make their judgments. They tend to pay careful attention to acts that are about to be performed. In many cases, their judgments prove to be right.

2. Erroneous Conscience: Erroneous conscience leads some people to make incorrect judgments. When something is bad, they think it is good and when it is good, they think it is bad. These people may not be acting in error maliciously, but there could be a defect in their intellect that leads them to make erroneous judgments. Their moral formation may also be defective.

3. Certain Conscience: This is when someone makes a judgement about whether a situation or an event, a person or an action is good or bad, right or wrong without fear of any possible mistake. When the intellect judges the morality of a specific action with a great

---

[109] Found in the *Catholic Encyclopedia*. "Catholic Encyclopedia: Synderesis" Retrieved 2 January 2016. Synderesis, or more correctly synteresis, is a term used by the Scholastic theologians to signify the habitual knowledge of the universal practical principles of moral action.

amount of certitude, that judgment should always be made. The popular principle is that "certain conscience" must always be followed. This comes from the moral principle that 'one must do good and avoid evil.' Now one may ask, what is that which directs the conscience to reach certitude? The natural law has been accepted by a great majority of people as the foundation for "certain conscience".

4. Doubtful Conscience: This is the conscience which dictates to the intellect that judgement on the moral goodness or evil of an action should be suspended. This is because the intellect is not able to see clearly whether the action is good or bad. In this situation, it is not wise to make any judgment. The person needs to gather more evidence for a prospective judgement. Strictly speaking, the term "doubtful conscious" is contradictory in the sense that it signifies a non-existent judgment. A more appropriate term could be "moral doubt". A doubtful conscience should not be followed for it entails the possibility of doing something wrong, bad or evil. The doubtful element must be resolved before an action is taken. However, a person has a moral responsibility to find ways of resolving his or her doubts.

A more serious situation could arise in connection with the faculty of judgment. The intellect could get used to issuing defective or biased judgments on the goodness or badness of actions. This may become habitual (or a way of life) for certain individuals. These two types of biases are what are call the "scrupulous conscience" and the "lax conscience."

1. Scrupulous Conscience: to scruple is to hesitate or be reluctant to do something that one thinks may be wrong. A scrupulous person sees evil where in fact there is no evil. He takes a lot of time and energy to decide to do something about which he is not sure whether it is right or wrong. This may be due to upbringing (sometimes by very strict parents who emphasize perfection in all actions).

2. Lax Conscience: This is the opposite of scrupulous conscience. People with this type of conscience tend to see no evil where in fact there is evil. These are morally disoriented persons. They are the people of whom we say in ordinary language that they

have "killed their conscience." These are the kind of people who may commit murder and go on living as if it is permissible to do so. The causes of lax conscience may a poor moral education, bad peer orientation, strong disorderly passions etc. People with a lax conscience are very dangerous to live with in a society. In addition, the situation may be even worse when the society does not recognize them.

3. Correct Conscience: This is the conscience that tells a person when something is good/correct or bad/wrong, and that perception is in agreement with what is objectively good/correct or bad/wrong. We have discussed how we reach this objectivity in chapter two. The natural law, which act as the foundation of correct moral conscience, will be discussed in the next chapter.

Having examined the seven different types of consciences, we shall now explore how the conscience is formed.

The Formation of Conscience

We start with a few very "existentialist questions": Can conscience be formed? And if so, who/what forms this conscience? What is the content of this formation? Since people are fallible and prone to error, it follows that they can err in matters of conscience. The possibility of falling into error prompts people to explore the formation of conscience. Today, due to the philosophical currents of subjectivism and relativism, many people tend to absolutize individual conscience. They claim that an action is good or bad simply because they think (or rather their conscience tells them) it is good or bad. They neglect the objective principles of morality.

Some of the consequences of this kind of thinking are: a breakdown in objective morality, increased violence in the streets, murder, premarital sex, extra-marital sex, early marriages, numerous divorces, looting, mob justice and so forth. This calls for the formation of conscience.

When we reflect accurately, we find that the environment in which we live influences our way of thinking. Friends (good or/and bad), schools, churches, literature such as books and newspapers, television, all these influence us. In the wake of the Covid-19 pandemic, the social media is continuing to influence us greatly. So too is the internet. Politicians, teachers, preachers and all types of professionals continue to influence our moral choices. We cannot escape this web of interconnectivity. All this reveals that our consciences are being formed (for better or worse) from different perspectives.

The formation of conscience is the process by which true principles of moral conduct gradually become operative in a person's mind, so that his mind gradually takes hold of these true principles. According to Sinag-Tala, the grasp of right principles is the first condition for the sound formation of conscience. But an equally important condition is to live according to these principles. In other words, conscience also tends to be formed by living according to conscience; and conscience tends to be deformed by living contrary to conscience. To hold certain principles in one's conscience, and then to act against them, is of the essence of moral evil.[110]

The strongest rival to the conscience is the will. Conscience can judge that something is good and that a good action needs to follow. On the other hand, the will can resist every effort of the conscience to do what it judges to be good. The fight may continue until one of the two wins. Sinag-Tala puts it like this:

Conscience judges that something is morally good, and ought to be done. For instance, a man feels he must tell the truth, even though, in his circumstances, he finds this very difficult. But the will is free. In his will, he may decide otherwise. He may choose to lie. To lie, of course, in such a case appears to the will as something good (not as a moral good, but as a good in the sense that it offers some immediate relief or satisfaction). Conscience may oppose this choice of the will, retaining a clear awareness that, at a deeper level, such a choice is not good. Or conscience may, after a debate, acquiesce for a moment, allowing that it seems good. But usually this acquiescence is short-lived. Once the will is satisfied in its object, its demands subside, the mind can review the situation in greater freedom and objectivity, and then conscience speaks with its voice of judgment:

---

[110] Sinag-Tala, *Conscience and Freedom, 2nd Edition*, (Manila: 1992)

'That was wrong'. And so the will stands accused. A man cannot shake off the awareness, 'I did wrong'.[111]

Formation of Conscience in the Catholic Church

Each tradition and culture has its own way of forming conscience. In the Catholic Church, the guidelines for the formation of conscience are well laid down in the Catechism of the Catholic Church (CCC).

I now present in summary form what the CCC says about the formation of conscience. The Catechism is prepared in article form and so it is easy for reader to find the references. The numbers in brackets refer to the reference numbers in the CCC. The three most important documents (on Conscience) which came from Second Vatican Council (1964) are *Gaudium et Spes* (GS), *Dignitatis Humanae* (DH*)* and *Lumen Gentium* (LG). These three documents are essential in understanding the teaching of the Catholic Church in matters pertaining to conscience. But we cannot forget the "most holy book", the Bible, which is first resource in the order of formation of conscious.

There follow in point form (without further explanation) some articles from CCC which speak about conscience.

The Judgment of Conscience

1. Deep within his conscience man discovers a law which he has not laid upon himself but which he must obey. Its voice, ever calling him to love and to do what is good and to avoid evil, sounds in his heart at the right moment (1776).

2. Moral conscience, present at the heart of the person, enjoins him at the appropriate moment to do good and to avoid evil (1777, see also Cf. *Rom* 2:14-16). It also judges particular choices, approving those that are good and denouncing those that are evil (1777 see also Cf. *Rom* 1:32).

3. Conscience is a judgment of reason whereby the human person recognizes the moral quality of a concrete act that he is going

---

[111] Sinag-Tala, *Conscience and Freedom.*

to perform, is in the process of performing, or has already completed (1778).

4. In all he says and does, man is obliged to follow faithfully what he knows to be just and right. It is by the judgment of his conscience that man perceives and recognizes the prescriptions of the divine law (1778)

5. It is important for every person to be sufficiently present to himself in order to hear and follow the voice of his conscience. This requirement of *interiority* is all the more necessary as life often distracts us from any reflection, self-examination or introspection (1779).

6. The dignity of the human person implies and requires *uprightness of moral conscience*. Conscience includes the perception of the principles of morality (synderesis); their application in the given circumstances by practical discernment of reasons and goods; and finally, judgment about concrete acts yet to be performed or already performed (1780).

7. The truth about the moral good, stated in the law of reason, is recognized practically and concretely by the *prudent judgment* of conscience. We call that man prudent who chooses in conformity with this judgment (1780).

8. Conscience enables one to assume *responsibility* for the acts performed. If man commits evil, the just judgment of conscience can remain within him as the witness to the universal truth of the good, at the same time as the evil of his particular choice (1781).

9. The verdict of the judgment of conscience remains a pledge of hope and mercy. In attesting to the fault committed, it calls to mind the forgiveness that must be asked, the good that must still be practiced, and the virtue that must be constantly cultivated with the grace of God (1781).

10. Man has the right to act in conscience and in freedom so as personally to make moral decisions. "He must not be forced to act contrary to his conscience. Nor must he be prevented from acting according to his conscience, especially in religious matters." (1782, see also *DH* 3 § 2).

The Formation of Conscience

1. Conscience must be informed and moral judgment enlightened. A well-formed conscience is upright and truthful. It formulates its judgments according to reason, in conformity with the true good willed by the wisdom of the Creator (1783).

2. The education of conscience is indispensable for human beings who are subjected to negative influences and tempted by sin to prefer their own judgment and to reject authoritative teachings (1783).

3. The education of the conscience is a lifelong task. From the earliest years, it awakens the child to the knowledge and practice of the interior law recognized by conscience (1784).

4. Prudent education teaches virtue; it prevents or cures fear, selfishness and pride, resentment arising from guilt, and feelings of complacency, born of human weakness and faults. The education of the conscience guarantees freedom and engenders peace of heart (1784).

5. In the formation of conscience the Word of God is the light for our path, we must assimilate it in faith and prayer and put it into practice (1785, see also Cf. *Ps* 119:105).

6. We must also examine our conscience before the Lord's Cross. We are assisted by the gifts of the Holy Spirit, aided by the witness or advice of others and guided by the authoritative teaching of the Church (1785, see also Cf. *DH* 14).

Erroneous Judgment

1. A human being must always obey the certain judgment of his conscience. If he were deliberately to act against it, he would condemn himself. Yet it can happen that moral conscience remains in ignorance and makes erroneous judgments about acts to be performed or already committed (1790).

2. This ignorance can often be imputed to personal responsibility. This is the case when a man "takes little trouble to find out what is true and good, or when conscience is by degrees almost blinded through the habit of committing sin." In such cases, the person is culpable for the evil he commits (1791, see also *GS* 16).

3. Ignorance of Christ and his Gospel, bad example given by others, enslavement to one's passions, assertion of a mistaken notion of autonomy of conscience, rejection of the Church's authority and her teaching, lack of conversion and of charity: these can be at the source of errors of judgment in moral conduct (1792).

4. If - on the contrary - the ignorance is invincible, or the moral subject is not responsible for his erroneous judgment, the evil committed by the person cannot be imputed to him. It remains no less an evil, a privation, a disorder. One must therefore work to correct the errors of moral conscience (1793).

5. A good and pure conscience is enlightened by true faith, for charity proceeds at the same time "from a pure heart and a good conscience and sincere faith." (1794, see also *1 Tim* 5; cf. 8:9; *2 Tim* 3; *1 Pet* 3:21; *Acts* 24:16).

6. The more a correct conscience prevails, the more do persons and groups turn aside from blind choice and try to be guided by objective standards of moral conduct (*GS* 16).

7. A human being must always obey the certain judgment of his conscience (1800).

Some Normative Underpinnings of Conscience

Modernity and its aftermath have led to the belief that conscience is a matter for individual persons and hence it has become a mere subjective affair. Some thinkers have argued that morality has nothing to do with conscience, hence the term at best can be perceived as neutral. The shift towards a normatively neutral understanding of conscience could have serious repercussions in the society. A simple definition of the term 'society' is 'the aggregate of people living together in a more or less ordered community'. 'Living together' implies the observance of law and order. If people were living individually, each in their own 'world' without social interaction, then rules cease to have any meaning. And in this kind of status-quo we can rightly talk of individual-subjective morality. We know very well that individuals are not isolated monads. They live in ordered and meaningful societies. The moment we enter into an ordinary society, in order to have cohesiveness, a call for objective morality is of paramount importance.

An example of this neutrality is found in an entry on conscience in the Stanford Encyclopedia of Philosophy. Alberto Giubilini conceives conscience 'like an empty box that can be filled with any type of moral content.'[112] This conception of conscience leaves the reader with many questions concerning morality. Can morality be justified from the convictions of conscience? Can morality be grounded in correct beliefs and values? Tom O'Shea challenges Giubilini's conception of conscience when he says, "this neutrality is almost always accompanied by an individualistic approach to conscience, which takes its proper content to be solely determined by each person for themselves."[113] This individualistic and egoistic application of conscience would lead to disfranchisement of the social ethos of any proper society.

Voltaire is of the opinion that in the absence of innate moral knowledge to guide conscience, it becomes 'necessary to instill just ideas and good principles into the mind.'[114] Many proponents of the natural law view of conscience acknowledge a role played by social relationships. It was Sorabji who noted that the innate disposition of conscience to recognize and kindle motivation by fundamental moral principles only becomes operative once we have been raised to adulthood or introduced to the relevant moral concepts.[115] Social structures help in the sharing of moral ideas and experiences which inform our thinking and acting. The social structures include family set up, religion, formal and informal education, sports activities, social and political gatherings. When these structures are well utilized and with a pure altruistic goal, they can become vital structures for the formation of conscience.

---

[112] Giubilini, Alberto, "Conscience", *The Stanford Encyclopedia of Philosophy* (Spring 2021 Edition), Edward N. Zalta (ed.), https://plato.stanford.edu/archives/spr2021/entries/conscience/

[113] Tom O'Shea, "Modern Moral Conscience", *Internal Journal of Philosophical Studies*, vol.26, 2018, https://www.tandfonline.com/doi/full/10.1080/09672559.2018.1497074

[114] Voltaire. 1901. "Conscience." In *Philosophical Dictionary*: Volume III. New York: DuMont. 234.

[115] Sorabji, R. *Moral Conscience through the Ages: Fifth Century BCE to the Present*, (Chicago: Chicago University Press, 2014) 62.

Lonergan: On Conscience

Conscience in Insight

Lonergan did not explicitly write on the 'notion of conscience' in his two major works (*Insight* and *Method*). The theme of moral conscience appears in chapter eighteen of *Insight* entitled "The Possibility of Ethics." It is here where Lonergan writes about the moral code and moral self-consciousness in the most general way. According to him, the content of the moral code is one thing, and the dynamic function that demands its observance is another.[116] Lonergan differs from Kant and Freud in the meaning he gives to the word "ought". He affirms a categorical imperative, but differs with Kant inasmuch as for him it is derived wholly from speculative intelligence and reason.[117] Lonergan, as opposed to Freud (who tried to overcome emotions and sentiments in his psychoneural therapy), believed that moral self-consciousness has a concomitant in moral emotions and moral sentiments.[118]

According to Lonergan, just as individuals can arrive at decisions which may be right or wrong, so too community decisions can be right or wrong. But in both cases, decisions are right or wrong not because of being pronounced by individual conscience, but because they are intelligent and reasonable in the concrete situation.

But just as individual intelligence and individual reasonableness lead to the individual decisions that may be right or wrong, so too common intelligence and common reasonableness lead to common decisions that may be right or wrong. Moreover, in both cases, decisions are right not because they are the pronouncements of the individual conscience, nor because they proceed from this or that type of social mechanism for reaching common decisions, but because they are in the concrete situation intelligent and reasonable. Again, in both cases, decisions are wrong, not because of their private

---

[116] *Insight*, 623.
[117] *Insight*, 624.
[118] *Insight*, 624.

or public origin, but because they diverge from the dictates of intelligence and reasonableness.[119]

Thus, intelligence and reasonableness become the guide for moral conscience. Lonergan again reminds the reader of the possibility of the three-fold bias - the individual, the group and the general bias that can prevent individuals and societies from reaching complete intelligence and reasonableness, which is necessary for proper moral conscience. He is aware that just as individuals, so too societies can fail to distinguish sharply and accurately between positions and counter-positions. As individuals, so also societies fail to reach the universal willingness that reflects and sustains the detachment and disinterestedness of the unrestricted desire to know.[120]

A Call for Authenticity in Method

The notion of authenticity in *Method* is given more prominence in the second chapter under the title "The Human Good." In the second part of "The Human Good", Lonergan dedicates much space to discussing the role of the feelings in the determination of judgments of value. He starts by acknowledging that we have feelings that are intentional responses and they answer to what is intended, apprehended, represented. Such feelings give intentional consciousness its mass, momentum, drive, power.[121] These feelings are very important in our knowing and deciding. Moreover, these are the feelings which drive us towards a world mediated by meaning. In line with Dietrich von Hildebrand's *Christian Ethics* (an expert in analyzing feelings), Lonergan has this to say,

> *We have feelings about other persons, we feel for them, we feel with them. We have feelings about our respective situations, about the past, about the future, about evils*

---

[119] *Insight*, 651.
[120] *Insight*, 651.
[121] *Method*, 30.

to be lamented or remedied, about the good that can, might, must be accomplished.[122]

Feelings that are intentional responses usually respond to values. They orient us towards self-transcendence. Lonergan trusts that feelings respond to values according to some scale of preference. He distinguishes vital, social, cultural, personal, and religious values in an ascending order.[123] Personal values and religious values are the key values in reaching authenticity. And what are they? "Personal value is the person in his self-transcendence, as loving and being loved, as originator of values in himself and in his milieu, as an inspiration and invitation to others to do likewise. Religious values, finally, are at the heart of the meaning and value of man's living and man's world."[124] Personal and religious values are at the core of our moral conscience. The ultimate challenge is to find a true criterion for orienting ourselves towards authentic personal and religious values. Lonergan gives a method for attaining true authenticity.

Lonergan reiterates that value is a transcendental notion. It is what is intended in questions for deliberation, just as the intelligible is what is intended in questions for intelligence, and just as truth and being are what are intended in questions for reflection.[125] When someone asks whether something is truly good or apparently good, or whether it is worthwhile or not, that person does not yet know value, but he/she is intending value. Transcendental notions provide criteria for reaching authenticity. Thus, Lonergan contends,

> *Not only do the transcendental notions promote the subject to full consciousness and direct him to his goals. They also provide the criteria that reveal whether the goals are being reached. The drive to understand is satisfied when understanding is reached but it is dissatisfied with every incomplete attainment and so it is the source of ever further questions. The drive to truth*

---

[122] *Method*, 31.

[123] *Method*, 31.

[124] *Method*, 32. For more explanation about what personal and religious values mean, I encourage the reader to read chapter 4 of *Method*. At the same time, chapter 8 of this book on religious conversion may also be of help.

[125] *Method*, 34.

compels rationality to assent when evidence is sufficient but refuses assent and demands doubt whenever evidence is insufficient. The drive to value rewards success in self-transcendence with a happy conscience and saddens failures with an unhappy conscience.[126]

Achieving self-transcendence is a long and painstaking process. It takes time to develop and reach to a sustained level of maturity. Since we live in a society, it demands a joint collaboration. On this issue, Lonergan make a final remark which summarizes the true meaning of authenticity. He strongly believes that only by reaching the sustained self-transcendence of the virtuous man that one becomes a good judge, not on this or that human act, but on the whole range of human goodness.[127] The criterion for true judgments of value remains the self-transcendence of the subject. Lonergan, as a believer, still had to show how the summit of authenticity is reached and where deep-seated and solid peace is to be found. He expressed it like this:

There are to be found the deep-set joy and solid peace, the power and the vigor, of being in love with God. In the measure that that summit is reached, then the supreme value is God, and other values are God's expression of his love in this world, in its aspirations, and in its goal. In the measure that one's love of God is complete, then values are whatever one loves, and evils are whatever one hates so that, in Augustine's phrase, if one loves God, one may do as one pleases, Ama Deum et fac quod vis. Then affectivity is of a single piece. Further developments only fill out previous achievement. Lapses from grace are rarer and more quickly amended.[128]

For a believer, God becomes the supreme value and other values are God's expression of his love in this world. Is there a better

---

[126] *Method*, 35. On the precise meaning of sufficient and insufficient evidence, see *Insight*, Chapters Ten and Eleven. I have also outline this meaning in chapter two above.

[127] *Method*, 35.

[128] *Method*, 39.

conscience than that which emanates from being truly in love with God? Is there a better criterion of achieving self-transcendence than falling truly in love with God?

Lonergan's Contribution

1. Most philosophers disregard the role of feelings in reasoning. Lonergan demonstrates how the intentional-response feelings (the detached, disinterested feelings as opposed to self-regarding feelings) enhance our rational conscience in the determination of judgments of value.

2. The presence of individual and group bias (we shall get more understanding in chapter 7) can prevent our conscience from making proper moral choices.

3. Lonergan demonstrates the criterion for reaching moral authenticity. It is only achieved through a painstaking process of self-transcendence. It is when we reach a desired level of maturity in self-transcendence that we can become good judges of our moral actions. It is this happy conscience that is able to choose correctly true human goodness.

4. An authentic conscience will always be directed by the supreme value. For the believers, this supreme value is none other than God.

Concluding Remarks and Suggestions

1. There is a good number of people who think that conscience is an "inner voice" telling a person what to do and what to avoid. In our analysis we have shown that this is not the case. Conscience in the strictest sense is a faculty (in the intellect) of moral judgment that distinguishes between right and wrong.

2. The scholastics had a closely related term – *Synderesis*. It is the innate principle in the moral consciousness of every person that directs the agent to good and restrains him from doing evil. This implies that in each one of us, there is an innate principle which in one way or another directs our actions.

3. Although Lonergan has not written explicitly on conscience, he gives a powerful method of understanding what true conscience means and the criterion for reaching authenticity in our moral judgments.

4. In almost all religions, there seems to be a consensus that our conscience takes its foundation from the natural law.

5. We suggest the following:
    a. We should make value judgements only when we are in certain conscience and correct conscience.
    b. We should refrain from making value judgements when we are in doubtful conscience.
    c. We need to undergo some formation of conscience in order to remain in certain and correct conscience.
    d. In case we realize that we have tendencies to either lax or scrupulous conscience, we should not hesitate to seek for professional help.

In the next chapter, we shall venture into a discussion of natural law from the historical perspective.

Case Study 4: False Witness

Gabriel has been in prison for the last twenty years in a certain country. He was accused of raping his 10-year-old daughter. The penalty for raping a minor in this country is life-imprisonment. However, after an appeal by the lawyers of Gabriel, the daughter confesses that she was coerced by her mother to give false evidence so that her father would be jailed. Her mother wanted to possess some real estate owned by her husband. The court releases Gabriel but tells him that further investigations will be carried out to establish his innocence. Outside the court, Gabriel embraces his daughter and tells her that he has forgiven her.

Questions for Deliberation

1. Gabriel's conscience: if he is truly innocent, what do you think he has been meditating on in prison for the last twenty years? Revenge, anger, hatred?
2. Gabriel's wife conscience: if it is true that she conspired with her daughter to falsely accuse her husband, what do you think has been going on in her mind for the past twenty years? Feeling guilty? Feeling sad?
3. Gabriel's daughter conscience: if it is true that she gave false witness, do you think she has been at peace for the last twenty years?
4. What do you think might have prompted Gabriel's daughter to confess her mistake?
5. What could have made Gabriel forgive his daughter after serving twenty years in jail?

V. The Natural Law

Again, natural laws are not to be determined by pure speculation but solely by an empirical method in which what is grasped by insight is mere hypothesis until confirmed by verification. Finally, the possible courses of action grasped by practical insight are merely possible until they are motivated by reflection and executed by decision.[129]

Questions for Reflection
1. What do you understand by natural law?
2. Do you think the actions of human beings are motivated by natural law?
3. Do you think there is a relationship between natural law and divine law?

Introduction

The natural law (as used in the philosophical arena) finds its roots in ancient Western philosophy. The earliest Greek cosmologists had to ask the ultimate and necessary question of the *urstoff* of the universe. They were searching for the principles that governed the entire cosmos which includes the *homo sapiens*. The Sophists made a clear distinction between nature *(physis, φύσις)* and law *(nomos, νόμος)*. According to the Sophists, what the law commanded could vary from place to place, but what nature commanded was the same and binding everywhere.

---

[129] *Insight*, 643.

It was during the scholastic period that the concept of natural law received its fine-tuning from mediaeval thinkers such as Albert the Great and St. Thomas Aquinas.

Natural law (*ius naturale, lex naturalis* in Latin*)* has been defined as a system of law based on a close observation of human nature, and on values intrinsic to human nature that can be deduced from and applied independently of the positive law (laws of a state).[130] The modern natural law theories were developed much later during the Age of Enlightenment.

Historical Exploration

Plato

Plato did not explicitly use of the tern "natural law" (except a brief mention in *Gorgias* 484 and *Timaeus* 83e). However, his concept of nature contains some of the elements found in many natural law theories. Plato believed that we live in an orderly universe. He sought to discover the basis of this orderly universe. He was convinced that the *forms* and especially the *form of the good*, which he calls "the brightest region of Being"[131] are the basis of this orderly universe. According to Plato, this *form* has to be sought at all time because it is the cause of all things and when it is seen, it leads a person to act wisely. And in his *Symposium* Plato identifies "the good" closely with the Beautiful. He narrates how Socrates' experience of the Beautiful enabled him resist the temptations of wealth and sex.[132] In the *Republic*, Plato is convinced that the ideal community is "a city which would be established in accordance with nature."[133] From Plato's works, we can easily deduce that he was convinced that there was a natural force which directed the orderly

---

[130] Finnis, John, "Natural Law Theories", *The Stanford Encyclopedia of Philosophy* (Summer 2020 Edition), Edward N. Zalta (ed.), https://plato.stanford.edu/archives/sum2020/entries/natural-law-theories/

[131] Plato, *The Republic,* 518b–d.

[132] Plato, *Symposium,* 211d–e.

[133] Plato, *The Republic*, 428e9.

universe. This natural force had to be obeyed by all human beings for the sake of the cohesion of a society.

Aristotle

Aristotle is sometimes thought of as the father of "natural law" theory. There is no real evidence for this distinction, but one thing is clear. St. Thomas in his elaboration of the natural law uses Aristotle quite often. This could be the reason why Aristotle has been viewed as the father of the natural law theory. However, there is some doubt as to whether St. Thomas correctly interpreted Aristotle on his (Aristotle's) thought concerning the natural law. Some philosophers have argued that Aristotle might not have used the term "natural law" as we understand it today. The idea of Aristotle having discovered natural law comes from his *Rhetoric*. In *Rhetoric*, we hear Aristotle saying that apart from the "particular laws" that each people have set for themselves, there is a "common law" that is according to nature.[134] It is here that we find Aristotle quoting Sophocles and Empedocles as he explains that "universal law is the law of nature. For there really is, as everyone to some extent divines, a natural justice and injustice that is binding on all men, even on those who have no association or covenant with each other... Not of today or yesterday it is, but lives eternal: none can date its birth."[135] Aristotle wants the reader to understand that human beings are all under the natural law. All creatures are subordinate to it. And, therefore, all have to obey it. Another important point that Aristotle also wants to emphasize is that this law has no beginning or end, and therefore it is eternal.

The Stoics

Another philosophical school of interest in the matter of "natural law" is Stoicism. It is a school of Hellenistic philosophy founded by Zeno of Citium in Athens in the early 3rd century BC. It

---

[134] Aristotle, *Rhetoric* 1373b2–8.
[135] Aristotle, *Rhetoric, Book I* – Chapter 13.

is a philosophy of personal ethics informed by its own system of logic and its views on the natural world.

According to its teachings, the path to *eudaimonia* (happiness, or blessedness) for social beings, is found in accepting each moment as it presents itself. One should not allow oneself to be controlled by the desire for pleasure or by the fear of pain. One should endeavor to use one's mind to understand the world and to play one's part in nature's plan by working together and treating others fairly and justly. According to stoicism, to live a good life, one had to understand the rules of the natural order since the Stoics thought everything was rooted in nature.

The Stoics also asserted the existence of a rational and purposeful order to the universe. There is a belief that Stoics believed that God is everywhere and in everyone (classical pantheism). According to this belief, within human beings there is a "divine spark" which helps them to live in accordance with nature. The Stoics felt that there was a particular way in which the universe had been designed, and that natural law helped human beings to live in harmony with themselves and with nature.

Marcus Tullius Cicero

Marcus Tullius (famously known as Cicero) of Ancient Rome wrote in *De Legibus* that both justice and law originate from what nature has given to humanity, from what the human mind embraces, from the functions of humanity, and from what serves to unite humanity.[136] For Cicero, natural law obliges us to contribute to the general good of the larger society. According to him, the purpose of positive laws is to provide for the safety of citizens, the preservation of states, and the tranquility and happiness of human life. Law, according to Cicero, "ought to be a reformer of vice and an incentive to virtue"[137] Cicero's conception of natural law reappeared in later centuries notably through the writings of St. Isidore and the Decretum of Gratian. St. Thomas Aquinas, in his summary of

---

[136] Cicero, *De Legibus*, bk. 1, sec. 16–17.

[137] Cicero, *De Legibus* (Keyes translation), bk. 1, sec. 58.

medieval natural law, quoted Cicero's statement that "nature" and "custom" were the sources of a society's laws.[138]

St. Thomas Aquinas

It was in the twelfth century that Gratian[139] equated the natural law with divine law. A century later, Albert the Great would address the subject, and his pupil, St. Thomas Aquinas, would restore Natural Law to its independent state. To do this he had to make a completely new formulation of the natural law. In his *Summa Theologica* Thomas asserted that natural law is the rational creature's participation in the eternal law.[140] Aquinas taught that all human or positive laws were to be judged by their conformity to the natural law. He strongly maintained that natural law meant "Good is to be sought, evil avoided."[141] According to Aquinas, human reason could not fully comprehend the eternal law and therefore it needed to be supplemented by revealed divine law. Aquinas explained that "there belongs to the natural law, first, certain most general precepts, that are known to all; and secondly, certain secondary and more detailed precepts, which are, as it were, conclusions following closely from first principles. As to those general principles, the natural law, in the abstract, can nowise be blotted out from men's hearts."[142] The above is a summary of the thought of Aquinas on natural law.

Other Scholastic thinkers who emphasized divine will instead of divine reason as the source of natural law include the Franciscan philosophers John Duns Scotus (1266–1308) and William of Ockham

---

[138] Thomas Aquinas, *Treatise on Law* edited by Stanley Parry (Chicago: Henry Regnery Company, 1969) 18 See also *Summa Theologica*, Questions 90–97.

[139] The *Decretum Gratiani* is a collection of canon law compiled and written in the 12th century as a legal textbook by the jurist known as Gratian. It forms the first part of the collection of six legal texts, which together became known as the Corpus Juris Canonici. It was used by canonists of the Roman until the Decretals, promulgated by Pope Gregory IX in 1234, obtained legal force. See "Decretals of Gregory IX". Code of Canon Law - IntraText. Retrieved 24 May 2020.

[140] *Summa Theologica*, I-II, Q.91, Art.2.

[141] *Summa Theologica*, I–II, Q. 94, Art. 2.

[142] *Summa Thelogica* I–II, Q. 94, A. 6.

(*c.* 1285–1347/49), and the Spanish theologian Francesco Suarez (1548–1617).

In short, natural law according to Aquinas has the following characteristics:

      a. It is given by God (divine origin)
      b. It is naturally authoritative over all human beings
      c. It is naturally knowable by all human beings
      d. It upholds that "the good" is prior to the right

The Idea of Natural Goodness

One of the recent entries in the Standard Encyclopedia of Philosophy is an article entitled "The Natural Law Tradition in Ethics" by Murphy Mark.[143] One of his subsections is "The Natural Goodness." Below are some of the important elements of the natural goodness, which he highlights in his article. He starts by asking two fundamental questions: 1. How is universal, natural goodness possible? 2. Given the variability of human tastes and desires, how could there be such universal "goods"? The two questions are very relevant in the contemporary situation that is characterized by autonomy, relativism and individualism. People want to choose their own good, their own desires, and their own tastes. Mark is of the opinion that natural law theorists have three answers to the two questions. He calls the first answer "the Hobbesian answer, based on a subjectivist theory. According to subjectivist theories of the good", what makes it true that something is good is that it is desired, or liked, or in some way is the object of one's pro-attitude, or would be the object of one's pro-attitudes in some suitable conditions.[144]

The second answer to the two questions above is Aristotelian. The idea here is to reject a subjectivism about "the good", holding that what makes it true that something is good is not that it stands in some relation to desire, but rather that it is somehow *perfective* or

---

[143] Murphy, Mark, "The Natural Law Tradition in Ethics", *The Stanford Encyclopedia of Philosophy* (Summer 2019 Edition). Cited hereafter as Mark, "The Natural Law Traditions."

[144] Mark, "The Natural Law Traditions."

completing of a being, where what is perfective or completing of a being depends on that being's nature.[145] Mark gives some examples as aids to clarifying what Aristotle meant by 'completing' and 'perfective.' He comments,

> *So what is good for an oak is what is completing or perfective of the oak, and this depends on the kind of thing that an oak is by nature; and what is good for a dog is what is completing or perfective of the dog, and this depends on the kind of thing that a dog is by nature; and what is good for a human depends on what is completing or perfective of a human, and this depends on the kind of thing a human is by nature.*[146]

Taking Aristotle's perfective theory, we find that, as "the good" is not defined fundamentally by reference to desire, the fact of variation in desire is not enough to raise questions about universal "goods". "The good" is determined in terms of the human nature. This view is also affirmed by St. Thomas and many other proponents of the natural law theory.

The third answer to the questions of natural goodness is Platonic. Like the Aristotelian view, it rejects a subjectivism about "the good". But it does not hold that "the good" is to be understood in terms of human nature. The role of human nature is not to define or set "the good", but merely to define what the possibilities of human achievement are. So one might think that some things – knowledge, beauty, etc. – are just good in themselves, apart from any reference to human desire or perfection, but hold that the pursuit of these is only part of the natural law insofar as they fall within the ambit of human practical possibility.[147] Therefore, according to Plato, "the good" is in things by themselves, and one has to find out what is that which is good in things.

None of the three answers given above went unchallenged. The Hobbesian view was rejected by many as too subjectivistic and because moral rules cannot hold universally if they are founded on

---

[145] Mark, "The Natural Law Traditions."
[146] Mark, "The Natural Law Traditions."
[147] Mark, "The Natural Law Traditions."

subjective grounds. The Platonic view was challenged on the basis that it is too metaphysical to be defensible and does not fit well with a conception of ethics grounded in nature. The Aristotelian view was also held to be too metaphysical in its orientation. However, most contemporary law theories are in line with the Aristotelian model of understanding the natural goodness.

Transition from "the good" to "the right"

We now have an idea of what is "the good" according to various theories. But how do we pursue that good? Contemporary society presents situations in which various different courses of action that can be pursued, each of which promises to realize some good. Are there some guidelines to which we might appeal in order to show some of these paths are more worthwhile than others? Is there a criterion of knowing how to pursue genuine "goods"?

According to Mark, there are three possibilities: the *master rule*, the *method approach* and the *virtue approach*. The *master rule* of right generates further rules. The *methodological principle* is that by which particular rules can be generated. In the *virtue approach*, one appeals to some standard for distinguishing correct from incorrect moral rules.[148] Let us now try to understand what the three approaches mean.

Using the *master rule* approach, the task of the natural law theorist is to identify some master rule which bears on the basic "goods" and, perhaps in conjunction with further factual premises, is able to produce a stock of general rules about what sorts of responses to the basic "goods" are or are not reasonable. It seems Aquinas employed this master rule approach. He held that this *master rule* is the rule of universal love, that one should love one's neighbor as oneself. This rule bids us to respond to "the good" lovingly wherever it can be realized, and from it we can see that certain ways of responding to "the good" are ruled out as essentially unloving. According to Mark, the central difficulty with the use of the master rule approach is that of explaining how we are to grasp this first

---

[148] Mark, "The Natural Law Traditions."

principle of morality as correct. What is the relationship between our knowledge of the basic "goods" and our knowledge of the master rule?[149]

When using the *methodological approach*, by contrast, there is no need for a master principle that will serve as the basis for deriving some particular moral rules. The idea here is that the natural law theorist does not need a master rule but a test for distinguishing correct moral rules from incorrect ones. What would distinguish different uses of the *method approach* is their accounts of what features of a choice we appeal to in order to determine whether it is defective. The knowledge that we have to work on here is our knowledge of the basic "goods". If a certain choice presupposes something false about the basic "goods", then it responds defectively to them.[150] The justification of a moral rule can be proved by showing that it rules out only choices that presuppose something false about the basic "goods".

The *virtue approach* is more concrete than the *master rule* and the *methodological approaches*. It presupposes that there are a number of choice situations in which there is a right answer but that right answer is not dictated by any natural law rule or set of rules, but rather is grasped only by a virtuous and practically wise person. It is, however, open to the natural law theorist to use this appeal to the judgment of the practically wise person more widely, because he believes that the general rules concerning the appropriate response to the "goods" cannot be properly determined by any master rule or philosophical method, but can be determined only by an appeal to the insight of the person of practical wisdom. For instance, if it really is wrong in all cases to tell lies, as Aquinas has argued, our grasp of this moral truth is dependent on our possessing practical wisdom, or our being able to recognize the possessor of such practical wisdom. If such a person never tells lies, because she or he just sees that to tell lies would be to respond defectively to "the good", then that lying is always wrong is a rule of the natural law.[151]

---

[149] Mark, "The Natural Law Traditions."
[150] Mark, "The Natural Law Traditions."
[151] Mark, "The Natural Law Traditions."

One challenge to these various natural law attempts to explain the "right" in terms of the "good" denies that the natural law theorist can provide adequate explanations of the range of norms of right conduct for which moral theories ought to be able to provide explanations. That is, one might allow for the sake of argument the natural law theorist's identification of some range of human "goods", while denying that he or she can identify, and justify in natural law terms, adequately concrete modes of appropriate response to those "goods".

Mark concludes his article with an important note. He points out that the intrinsic moral authority of the natural law has been a matter of debate since Aquinas: it was a central issue dividing Aquinas's view from those of Scotus, Ockham, and Suarez.[152] Moreover, I would add that it continues to be a thorny issue among the natural law theorists up to the present.

Lonergan: A New Approach to Natural Law

Introduction

The term 'natural law' is not used very often in the two major works of Lonergan (*Insight* and *Method*). In *Insight* the term appears only once in the chapter of 'self-affirmation of the knower,' where Lonergan wants to emphasize that the self-affirmation itself is an immanent law. Here too, he makes it clear that the cognition process lies under the control of natural law.[153] In other parts of text he talks about "natural laws" (7 times) in the plural. Lonergan consistently states that natural laws are not to be determined by pure speculation but solely by an empirical method in which what is grasped by insight is mere a hypothesis until confirmed by verification.[154] It now becomes clear that Lonergan is offering a method to understand natural law.

The significant treatment of the natural law is found in his shorter papers written between 1974 to 1982. These papers were first

---

[152] Mark, "The Natural Law Traditions."
[153] *Insight*, 354.
[154] *Insight*, 643.

edited by Frederic E. Crowe and published in 1985 by Paulist Press. Later, the same papers were included in the critical edition by Robert M. Doran and John D. Dadosky in the series of the Collected Works of Bernard Lonergan, *A Third Collection*, Vol. 16. The specific paper in question is entitled 'Natural Right and Historical Mindedness'. This paper is arguably among Lonergan's most important shorter writings.[155]

Natural Right and Historical Mindedness

At the beginning of this short presentation of the new approach to the natural law by Lonergan, I would like to clarify his usage of the term 'natural right' in his lecture. According to Robert Doran, Lonergan was engaging with Leo Strauss and his disciples in this lecture. Strauss's work figured prominently in the intellectual atmosphere of Boston College, where Lonergan was teaching at that time. We find that one of the Strauss's more important books is entitled *Natural Right and History*. 'Natural right' was Strauss's term for what is more commonly called natural law.[156] From this, we can deduce that Lonergan refers to 'natural law' as 'natural right'. Lonergan is partly in agreement and partly not in agreement with Strauss's treatment of the natural law.

Lonergan's approach to the notion of natural law is quite different from the traditional approaches we have discussed above. He makes a shift from a classicist mentality to a historical mindedness. The classicists viewed reality in terms of their essences and natures. Consequently the immutability and the purported objectivity of any judgments were made from this way of perceiving them. The classicists were conservative and traditional.[157] They abstracted from the concrete in order to achieve abstract, universal

---

[155] Bernard Lonergan, *A Third Collection*, Collected Works of Bernard Lonergan, vol. 16, edited by Robert M. Doran and John D. Dadosky, (Toronto: University of Toronto Press, 2017) book jacket, front-inside. Cited hereafter as *A Third Collection*.

[156] This information is from one of the lectures of Robert Doran in the year 2006. It is entitled 'RGT 5572 HS, Class 8'. See also the first footnote under the title, 'Natural Right and Historical Mindedness' in *A Third Collection*, 163.

[157] Bernard Lonergan, *A Second Collection*, Collected Works of Bernard Lonergan, vol. 13, edited by Robert M. Doran and John D. Dadosky, (Toronto: University of Toronto Press, 2016) 4. Cited hereafter as *A Second Collection*.

norms. They were mainly guided by the abstract rules of logic and metaphysics. These norms were meant to ensure a degree of order in society.

Lonergan, on the other hand, considers the modern human being from the liberal and the historicist point of view. The two positions (classicist and liberal/historicist) differ in their apprehension of man and in their account of the "good". These are differences in horizon and in total mentality.[158]

The issue at hand is 'collective responsibility.' Is there anything like collective responsibility in the modern world which is infused with so much relativism and individualism? Lonergan observes that if collective responsibility is not yet an established fact, then it may be a possibility which can be realized. This possibility is desirable to realize.[159] To realize this possibility, Lonergan presents two elements which exist in our tradition – the notion of the natural right (or natural law) which originates from the ancient Greeks, and the human historicity (besides human nature) which emanates from the nineteenth century historical thought.[160] He tries to bring these two elements together. He wants to articulate a normative stance by showing how the notion of natural right (or natural law) is relevant to human historicity.

Lonergan makes a distinction between two components in concrete human reality: human nature which is constant, and human historicity which is variable. He says that nature is given at birth, and that which one makes of him/herself is the historicity. He is of the opinion that as we see changes in the development of the human being so too there are changes in social institutions. We all have to adapt to changing circumstances.[161] For Lonergan, all such change is in its essence a change of meaning – a change of idea or concept, a change of judgement or evaluation, a change of the order or the request.[162]

---

[158] *A Second Collection*, 4.
[159] *A Third Collection*, 164.
[160] *A Third Collection*, 164.
[161] *A Third Collection*, 164.
[162] *A Third Collection*, 164.

Why do we need that change? It is a change essentially in meaning. This change of meaning occurs in all levels of human existence. Lonergan expresses the significance of historicity on the cultural and social levels. And in all these levels, the cognitional process is at work. He expresses it thus,

> Human community is a matter of a common field of experience, a common mode of understanding, a common measure of judgment, a common consent. Such community is the possibility, the source, the ground of common meaning that is the form and act that finds expression in family and polity, in the legal and economic system, in customary morals and educational arrangements, in language and literature, art and religion, philosophy science, and the writing of history. Still community itself is not a necessity of nature but an achievement of man. Without a common field of experience, people get out of touch. Without a common mode of understanding, there arise misunderstanding, distrust, suspicion, fear, hostility, factions. Without common measure of judgment, people live in different worlds. Without common consent, they operate at cross-purposes. Then common meaning is replaced by different and opposed meanings.[163]

When the change of meaning is effected, all the social and economic dimensions of human living change as well. When one challenges the common meaning of the established social, cultural or economic structures, he/she challenges the achievements of these structures.

As seen above, human nature is a constant while historicity is a variable. How do we understand the variable? To understand the constant (human nature) one needs to study the individual human beings, but to understand the variable, historicity, one has to study each instance as it emerges. Lonergan borrows the phrase 'historical mindedness' from Alan Richardson; this term means that to understand men and their institutions, we have to study their

---

[163] *A Third Collection*, 164-65.

history.[164] For it is history that man's making of man occurs, that it progresses and regresses, that through such changes there may be discerned a certain unity in an otherwise disconcerting multiplicity.[165]

Now, what do we understand by 'nature'? Lonergan uses the definition of nature given by Aristotle as an immanent principle of movement and of rest. In man such a principle is the human spirit asking and answering questions. When asking questions, it is an immanent principle of movement. When answering questions and doing so satisfactorily, it is an immanent principle of rest.[166] It is at this point that Lonergan goes on to specify different types of questions which are found at the three levels of cognitional structure: the questions for intelligence, the questions for reflections and the questions for deliberation. It is in giving correct and meaningful answers to these questions in different instances that we can validly understand the meaning of natural right (or natural law).

The Dialectic of History

It is in the dialectic of history that one finds the link between natural right and historical mindedness. The source of natural right lies in the norms immanent in human intelligence, human judgment, human evaluation, human affectivity.[167] Lonergan gives certain elements to understand the dialectic of human history under six headings[168] which I summarize in the following six statements.

1. Human meanings develop in human collaboration. There is the expansions of social meanings in the evolution of domestic, economic and political arrangements.

2. Such expansions occur on a succession of plateaus. They start from the most primitive stages and move to the most advanced. This development is mainly of practical intelligence, and its style is the

---

[164] *A Third Collection*, 165.
[165] *A Third Collection*, 165.
[166] *A Third Collection*, 166.
[167] *A Third Collection*, 170.
[168] *A Third Collection*, 170-176.

spontaneous accumulation of insights into the ways of nature and the affairs of men. There is also awareness of the cosmos.

3. Attention shifts beyond developments in doing and in speaking to developments generally. The central concern is with human understanding where developments originate, with the methods used in natural science and in critical history which chart the course of discovery and, more fundamentally, with the generalized empirical method that underpins both the scientific and empirical method that supplies philosophy with a basic cognitional theory, an epistemology and, by a way of corollary, with a metaphysics of proportionate being. On this plateau, logic loses its key position and becomes but a modest part within method; and logical concern – with truth, with necessity, with demonstration, with universality – enjoys no more than a marginal significance. Science and history become ongoing processes, asserting not necessities but verifiable possibility, and claiming not certitude but probability.

4. Then there is the critique of our historicity, of what our past has made us. This will be an ongoing task. It will be an empirical task but one within the orbit of human studies and thus concerned with the operative meanings constitutive of our social arrangements and cultural intercourse.

5. The dialectic of historicity will deal with the ambiguity of completeness or incompleteness of plateaus in the context of meaning or action.

6. Beyond dialectic, there is dialogue. While the dialectic of history coldly relates our conflicts, dialogue adds the principle that prompts us to cure them, the natural right that is the inmost core of our being.

Finally, Lonergan makes it clear that whole movement is an ongoing process of self-transcendence. For self-transcendence reaches its term not in righteousness but in love, and when we fall in love, then life begins anew. A new principle takes over, and as long as it lasts, we are lifted above ourselves and carried along as parts within an ever more intimate yet ever more liberating dynamic whole.[169]

Lonergan's Contribution

1. In his new version of the natural law, Lonergan presents the modern human being from the liberal and the historicist point of view. Though human nature remains the same in every epoch, the historicity is dynamic and keeps on changing. This underlines for us that the normativity of the natural law has to be perceived according to the signs of the times.

2. It is only by asking the correct questions (and giving the correct answers) which occur at the three levels of cognitional structure (the questions for intelligence, questions for reflections and questions for deliberation) that we can discover the true meaning of the natural law.

3. Finally, Lonergan demonstrates to us that natural law can only be fully understood in self-transcendence. The natural law is not something to be learnt by the human mind, but it is something to be articulated by the heart, by falling in love unconditionally.

Concluding Remarks and Suggestions

1. One of the factors that makes the natural law relevant even in the contemporary society is that it seems to offer a clear moral criterion for a world which is disfranchised and distressed by moral obscurities and deviations.

2. It is not just optimism to conclude that we live in an orderly universe. It is a matter of fact that the nature has a way of ordering things. We see climatic cycles of the year occurring systematically. We see animals give birth to young ones which resemble their mothers perfectly. These young ones grow to maturity and in their turn give birth to young ones of the same nature. And the cycle

---

[169] *A Third Collection*, 169.

continues. This reveals that there must be some intrinsic principles which control the nature.

3. The advancement of science and technology is, in many cases, good for human beings. Modern science has proved that man's intellect is capable of 'modifying the nature' (what I mean here is trying to modify things in nature in order to get something which seems to be of higher/better quality, such us GMOs). Whether 'modifying the nature' is morally good/permissible is a point of debate. Secondly, whether 'modifying the nature' would mean going against the natural law is also a point of debate. This 'modification of the nature' has proved to have some adverse consequences to humanity.

4. Believers in transcendental being have highly regarded natural law as the foundational and main guide to moral truth. A great majority of the believers in transcendental being hold that natural law is the main cause and guide for moral consistency.

5. We suggest the following:
   a. That we have a positive outlook towards the nature of the universe in totality (the total ecosystem in which human beings are a part).
   b. That we learn to respect and obey the natural law (the moral standard that govern human behavior, eg., it is natural that killing human being is wrong). In doing so we perfect our being – the humanness.
   c. That we learn to ask the right questions concerning the universe of being in order to discover the true meaning of the natural law.

The next chapter will challenge us to ask one of the most basic questions, "Are we free in our moral choices?"

Case Study 5: Same Sex Marriage

In an argument marked by sharp exchanges on the consequences of its decision establishing a right to same-sex marriage, the Supreme Court considered whether city X may bar a Catholic agency that refuses to work with same-sex couples from screening potential foster parents. Chief Justice P, who dissented from the decision, asked a lawyer for the agency, Catholic Social Services, whether her client's position, rooted in religious freedom, was "in tension with another set of rights, those recognized in our decision." Justice Q. did indeed call for "an open and searching debate" on same-sex marriage.

The city barred Catholic Social Services from screening potential foster parents after a certain magazine described its policy against placing children with same-sex couples. The agency and several foster parents sued the city, seeking for justice. They said the city's action violated their first amendment rights to religious freedom and free speech.

Questions for Deliberation
1. In the case above, do you think the natural law is applicable?
2. In your own judgement, was the natural law violated in any way?
3. Could the natural law be used to justify any aspect of the case?
4. Do you think the Catholic Social Services was morally consistent in their decision?

VI. Freedom and Responsibility

The most obvious bit of evidence for the freedom of man's decisions lies in the possibility of inconsistency between human knowing and doing; for if such inconsistency is possible, then there cannot be any valid argument from determinate knowing to determinate willing and doing. However, one is not to mistake the obvious for the essential. Man is not free because he can be unreasonable in his choices. Rather the root of freedom lies in the contingence of the formal intelligibility of proportionate being.[170]

Questions for Reflection

1. What do you understand by "freedom"?
2. What is "essential freedom"?
3. What is "effective freedom"?
4. What directs your making of choices?

Introduction

Freedom is one of the most discussed topics in contemporary society. Everybody claims to know what freedom is. Everyone wants to be free. We want to live and work in an atmosphere of freedom. But do we really know what true freedom is? To what extent can we claim to be free? Is there a limit to our freedom? Is absolute freedom attainable? When we talk of freedom, are we thinking of responsibility?

---

[170] *Insight*, 644.

People want freedom but without taking responsibility for their actions. Perhaps the major problem lies in the separation of the two terms: freedom and responsibility.

Analogous Meanings of the Word 'Freedom'

The Merriam Webster dictionary defines "freedom" as the quality or state of being free, such as the absence of necessity, coercion, or constraint in choice or action. This is the plain meaning of the word "freedom". We have other meanings that we attach to the term 'freedom.' In the sovereign democracies, freedom is liberation from slavery or restraint from the power of another. Thus, we talk of independent states. People talk of freedom of choice (the ability to make their own choices), freedom of speech and of thought (the ability to say or think whatever they want), freedom of information (information to be given to whoever wants it), freedom of worship (the ability to choose the object of worship and the expression of the same), freedom from injustice (the condition of not having to suffer injustices) and many other such expressions of freedom.

We can also talk of freedom in various existential spheres of life such as social freedom (interacting with one another without restrictions), economic freedom (allowing ownership and encouraging stewardship, free trade etc.), and political freedom (civil liberty, the ability to exercise democratic rights etc.). Parents would like to see their children grow in a responsible freedom, while children would like to be given space to exercise their freedom. All this reveals that people have attached various meanings to the word 'freedom.'

Some preliminary questions come to mind: To what extent are human beings free? Can a prisoner be said to be free while serving his/her jail sentence? Are the students in day schools freer than those in boarding schools? Are the children of *laisse faire* parents freer than those of strict parents? Are the citizen of more democratic governments freer than those of less democratic governments? Can we talk of animals being "free"? Can God be described as "free"? These are important questions which can be answered only by a deep reflection on the true meaning of freedom. The process of self-appropriation will be of great help in delving into these existential questions.

Let us recapitulate what we presented in chapter one. We described how in the pre-Sophistic era, there was no real distinction between the *phusis* (nature or the laws of nature) and the *nomos* (human convention). Thus, humanity was identified with nature. That being the case, the human mind was totally under the control of nature. And therefore, we could not rightly talk of free choice. It was the Sophists who made a real distinction between the *phusis* and the *nomos*, thus inaugurating the era of free choice. Plato (Socrates) went further to claim that only a knowledgeable person can be virtuous. He claimed that one cannot do wrong if one knows that it is wrong. He did not seem to have much regard for the freedom of choice. Though Aristotle recognized the difference between voluntary and involuntary actions in his *Nicomachean ethics*, he followed his master in disregarding the role of freedom in making choices. It was Aquinas who was responsible for a tremendous revolution in the understanding of freedom of choice by integrating virtue and intellect in making right judgments.

The Notion of Freedom in Lonergan

Introduction

The theme of 'freedom' has an early and indispensable place in the works of Bernard Lonergan. His doctoral dissertation (*Gracia Operans: A Study of the Speculative Development in the Writings of St. Thomas Aquinas*) which he completed in May 1940 at the Pontifical Gregorian University in Rome explored the theme of freedom. In 1971, the four articles from his dissertation that had been published earlier (in 1941-42) were collected together and published in book form under the title *Grace and Freedom: Operative Grace in the Thought of St. Thomas Aquinas*.[171] As Frederick E. Crowe noted,

---

[171] Bernard Lonergan, *Grace and Freedom: Operative Grace in the Thought of St. Thomas Aquinas*, Edited by Frederick E. Crowe and Robert M. Doran, Collected Works of Bernard Lonergan, Vol. 1, (Toronto: University of Toronto Press, 2000), xviii. Cited hereafter as *Grace and Freedom*.

Grace and Freedom (Vol. 1 of the Collected Works of Bernard Lonergan) represents Lonergan's entry into subject matter that would occupy him throughout his lifetime.[172] It is quite evident that Lonergan devoted a substantial amount of time to the examination of this theme of freedom in his later works, specifically in *Insight*.

I will present Lonergan's notion of freedom mainly from his work, *Insight*. In *Insight*, Lonergan treats the notion of freedom in chapter 18, 'The Possibility of Ethics.' At this point, the reader should be aware that Lonergan is offering a solid method for how to tackle fundamental issues affecting the human person. He has already offered a method for the study of cognitional theory, epistemology and metaphysics and now he offers a method in ethics. He is looking at the possibility of ethics. This is where he asks relevant questions such as, "Is man condemned to moral frustration? Is there a need for a moral liberation if human development is to escape the cycle of alternating progress and decline?"[173]

At the outset of the presentation of this important theme, Lonergan warns the reader that his concern is not to draw up a code of ethics but rather to answer the relevant prior questions.[174] By attempting to answer these relevant prior questions, Lonergan is offering a remote possibility of ethics through which he invites the readers (or his critics) to make a transition to proximate possibility. He put it thus,

> *I feel justified in expecting critics to suppose that readers of this book will be able to make the transition from the remote possibility of ethics, which is established, to the proximate possibility, which the exigent may demand.*[175]

By the phrase 'remote possibility of ethics,' Lonergan wants to indicate that he is assisting the reader in discovering a method to solve ethical issues. This method is in-built in each one of us. It issues from our rational self-consciousness. In his presentation about the notion of freedom, he will assist the reader in understanding what is

---

[172] *Grace and Freedom:* book jacket, front inside page.
[173] *Insight*, 618.
[174] *Insight*, 618.
[175] *Insight*, 618.

meant by rational self-consciousness. It is possible that in some instances we manage to make a transition from rational consciousness to rational self-consciousness, where we are required to make judgments of value on ethical issues. But we may lack the awareness of this transition. Let us now look into the nature of human freedom.

The Nature of Human Freedom

In his treatment of the nature of human freedom, Lonergan identifies four main elements namely, the underlying sensitive flow, the practical insight, the process of reflection, and the decision. The four elements correspond to the four transcendental precepts[176] namely, being attentive, being intelligent, being reasonable and being responsible. They, too, correspond to the process of reaching the judgment of fact, followed by the judgment of value. This shows the reader that in order to make an authentic judgment of value, there is a certain process which he/she must follow. We shall consider these four elements one by one.

The Underlying Sensitive Flow

Human beings have real feelings. These feelings enable human beings to interact with one another. Psychologists confirm if human beings are devoid of any feelings, then normal and ordinary life will be impossible. People will become like robots and will be performing their actions mechanically without regard for one another. According to Lonergan, the underlying sensitive flow consists of sensible presentations and imaginative representations of affective and aggressive feelings, of conscious bodily movements, etc.[177] In many cases we are conscious of these feelings which take place in ourselves. Psychic development has to take place in a normal way, at its own time and pace, if we are to function properly in our actions. At this level, the underlying drive is the affective drive and perhaps some strange feelings in us and, therefore, we cannot rightly talk of

---

[176] The transcendental precepts are explained by Lonergan in *Method*. For more understanding of what they mean, see *Method*, 20.

[177] *Insight*, 632.

the existence of free acts of will. We still need to appeal to some higher integration of intelligence.

The Practical Insight

This is the second element considered by Lonergan in the treatment of the human freedom. The practical insight follows from the sensitive flow of data. We need to understand our normal feelings. We need to distinguish between the self-regard feelings, and the detached and disinterested feelings. We need to grasp some intelligible unity in ourselves. In chapter two, we saw that beyond the question for intelligence that is met by insight, there is always the question for reflection. The question for reflection leads to the judgment of fact (that this is the case). Now, according to Lonergan, while speculative and factual insights are oriented to lead to knowledge of being, practical insights are oriented to lead to the making of being.[178] Practical insights lead to the pronouncement of the judgment of value. Their objective is not what is, but what is to be done. These judgements are geared to revealing possible causes of action. Again, we saw in chapter two that for a factual insight to be correct, it needs to reach a virtually unconditioned. (I refer the reader to chapter 2 for more understanding of the meaning of "virtually unconditioned"). This is not the case with practical insight. Here we are involved with a possibility not actuality. Therefore, a practical insight grasps only a possibility.

Practical Reflection

We move now to the third element which is the movement from practical insight to practical reflection. We have seen that the practical insight grasps the possibility of an action. This possibility may not necessarily result in automatic execution. Further relevant questions may still exist. This depends on the familiarity of the person with the issue at hand. The issue at hand may be so complicated that a person may hesitate to take responsibility for the possible consequences. There arises the willingness or unwillingness to pass judgement. Lonergan alludes to the fact that the essence of the reflection does not consist in the number of questions asked or in

---

[178] *Insight*, 633.

the length of time spent in reaching answers.[179] What is of paramount importance is "willingness". But willingness still has to come under scrutiny. Is that willingness right or wrong, good or bad?[180] This willingness has to become a habit. But perhaps this habit needs constant improvement. Now the question of value comes into play. Lonergan invites the reader to ask very imperative questions regarding value. "Are the values to which they commit me true or false? Am I intelligent and reasonable enough in the short run, only to be blind to the larger implications of my way of living? Or if I advert to such larger implications, am I doing what I can to be helpful to others in this respect?"[181] These are questions for practical reflection which lead the reader to make judgements of value. We need to evaluate our values. We need to constantly evaluate our way of living. It was Socrates who said that unexamined life is not worth living.[182]

Now practical reflection consists in an actuation of rational self-consciousness. I become rationally self-conscious inasmuch as I am concerned with the reasons for my own acts, and this occurs when I scrutinize the object and investigate the motives of a possible course of action.[183] Practical reflection is meant to go beyond mere knowing. It is one thing to know what is good, what is right, what is expected, what is worthwhile, but it is quite another for this knowledge to issue in right action. The practical reflection is completed only when it results in the right/wrong or correct/incorrect action. As long as I am reflecting, I have not yet reached my decision. What was mere possibility has now become an actuality.

The Decision

The fourth element in Lonergan's analysis of the notion of freedom is that of making the decision. According to Lonergan, decision is an act of willing. It is an act of willing because it possesses

---

[179] *Insight*, 633.

[180] *Insight*, 634.

[181] *Insight*, 634.

[182] I had already given this famous quote of Socrates in chapter one. See *Plato's Apology of Socrates*, 38a.

[183] *Insight*, 634.

internal mechanisms which pose alternatives for either consenting or refusing to consent.[184] This is the essence of human freedom. We have seen earlier that in order to reach a judgment of fact, there is a rigorous process of reflective understanding. There is a reflective grasp of reasons. When making a decision, the same process is followed. Both are rational and deal with objects apprehended by insight. Lonergan identifies a radical difference between the rationality of judgment and the rationality of decision. He expresses it thus:

> *Judgment is an act of rational consciousness, but decision is an act of rational self-consciousness. The rationality of judgment emerges in the unfolding of the detached and disinterested desire to know in the process towards knowledge of the universe of being. But the rationality of decision emerges in the demand of the rationally conscious subject for consistency between his knowing and his deciding and doing. Again, the rationality of judgment emerges if in fact a reasonable judgment occurs, but the rationality of decision emerges if in fact a reasonable decision occurs.*[185]

I'm certain each one of us had had an experience of making a decision. Lonergan has beautifully analyzed the whole process, right from the moment of raising an issue, to the moment of reflective understanding, in which after reaching a virtually unconditioned a person has no option but to pass a rational judgement. And he/she must go further to reach a self-rational consciousness which is needed to make a rational choice, to decide and then execute the decision. The radical challenge here is to be morally rational consistent. Is your knowing consistent with your choice and decision?

Finally, let me end this part of reflection with an example of my own self-appropriation. While I was pondering on Lonergan's thought and integrating it into my reflection, something happened to me. I felt dry in my mouth. Then I remembered that I had two sweets in my pocket. But I was not sure whether I had eaten them the

---

[184] *Insight*, 636.
[185] *Insight*, 636.

previous day or they were still in my pocket. Let us see how the whole process worked out. On the level of presentations (the underlying sensitive flow), I find myself feeling dry in my mouth. And when I remembered that there might be two sweets in my pocket I literally salivated. The reflective understanding (the practical insight in my consciousness) took place so fast and I found myself making a judgment of fact (practical reflection) that there were sweets in my pocket. I had to verify whether my insight (the practical insight) was correct by putting my hands in my pocket (back to sensitive flow). And I found it was true (practical reflection, after reaching a virtually unconditioned) that I had two sweets in my pocket. The judgment of fact was completed. Now I had to make a quick choice: should I chew the two sweets at once, or should I take one at a time, or should I wait and take both of them later? Then I asked a further question: Are these sweets good for my health at this time? After marshalling those few questions, I decided to eat one sweet (the decision). I had already reached rational self-consciousness and was willing to make a choice and to act. When I reflected on the whole process, I found myself consistent in the sense that my knowing was consistent with my choice and doing. I took the responsibility for the possible consequences[186] of my final decision. It is worth noting something important in my reflection. There were two distinct types of desires. In the first place, there was a desire to eat the sweet. This is a self-regarding desire and it is in the purely biological pattern of experience. In the second place, there was a pure desire to know whether I had sweets in my pocket (also to know whether eating sweets is good for my health or not). This desire is detached and disinterested, and it is in the intellectual pattern of experience. This is a simple rational reflection. There are more complex moral issues which may take longer to reach self-rational consciousness. What is more important is the awareness of the whole process that takes place, and the willingness to act according to the will. We shall now explore the notion of will.

---

[186] Whatever decision one takes, there are usually consequences. Consequences may be good or bad. Again, to be good or bad is a question of debate. This also depends on each one's value system. But there is what we may call 'objective good'. See the Lonergan's notion of the human good in chapter 2 of *Method* and also chapter 9 of this book.

The Notion of Will

Lonergan calls the will "intellectual or spiritual appetite."[187] It is a faculty in the intellect. It is the intellect that feeds the will. Whatever is presented to the intellect, the will decides to act on or not. In its native stage, the will needs to be tutored in order to acquire some mastery. When it acquires this mastery, then it can grasp readily the solution of any problem that arises. Just like the process of knowing, the will takes time to become habitual.

Lonergan is very careful with the use of his terms. He differentiates three very important aspects: the capacity is 'will', the habit is 'willingness' while the act is 'willing'.[188] The reader needs to be cautious when using these terms in the context of Lonergan's thought.

The act of willing is rational. We saw in chapter two that the unrestricted desire to know grasps intelligently and affirms reasonably the facts of universe of being. Further, this desire to know grasps intelligently and affirms reasonably not only the facts of the universe of being but also its practical possibilities. Lonergan reminds the reader that the human being is not only a knower, but also a doer. It is the same intelligent and rational consciousness that grounds the doing as well as the knowing.[189] He insists that there should be a consistency between knowing and doing. This consistency can be achieved only by a willing will. We all know very well that, in fact, moral living is not easy. A conscious effort has to be made by the will for a person to be consistent in moral living. Lonergan asks the reader to enter into his/her moral self-consciousness. This is the only remedy for inconsistency between knowing and doing. And this is the work of the faculty of the will.

Now let us deepen our understanding of the notion of the will. "Act of willing" is all about the actuation of rational self-consciousness. Lonergan explains how one reaches this actuation:

---

[187] *Insight*, 621.
[188] *Insight*, 622.
[189] *Insight*, 622.

I am empirically conscious inasmuch as I am experiencing, intellectually conscious inasmuch as I am inquiring or formulating intelligently, rationally conscious inasmuch as I am seeking to grasp the virtually unconditioned or judging on the basis of such a grasp. But I become rationally self-conscious inasmuch as I am concerned with reasons for my own acts, and this occurs when I scrutinize the object and investigate the motives of a possible course of action.[190]

Lonergan insists that a person can know clearly and distinctly what he/she ought to do. But it is only the act of willing which leads him/her to make a transition from knowing to doing. He stresses that,

though the reflection heads beyond knowing to doing, still it consists simply in knowing. Thus, it may reveal that the proposed action is concretely possible, clearly effective, highly agreeable, quite useful, morally obligatory, etc. But it is one thing to know exactly what could be done and all the reasons for doing it. It is quite another for such knowledge to issue in doing.[191]

What Lonergan points to in the above quotation is exactly what often happens in our daily discussions and evaluations. We hold meetings to plan and to evaluate our events. In many cases we find ourselves making very impressive plans for our activities. At the end of the year when we come to do an evaluation, we may be surprised to see that very little has been actualized. This is true also when we come to our personal lives. We may know clearly what is expected of us, but we may lack courage, determination and willingness to choose wisely in accordance to our value system and to make right decisions.

---

[190] *Insight*, 634.

[191] *Insight*, 634.

Essential and Effective Freedom

Lonergan wants the reader to understand clearly that there is a difference between essential and effective freedom. The two aspects are mutually inclusive. He writes,

> *Man is free essentially inasmuch as possible courses of action are grasped by practical insight, motivated by reflection, and executed by decision. But man is free effectively to a greater or less extent inasmuch as this dynamic structure is open to grasping, motivating, and executing a broad or a narrow range of otherwise possible courses of action.*[192]

A person may be essentially free to stop stealing but not effectively free to do so. This is one of the toughest challenges facing the existential subject. The subject may know clearly that he/she is involved in a morally wrong situation, but he/she may consciously decide not to change his/her wrongdoing.

The essential freedom sets the ground for effective freedom. There cannot be effective freedom without essential freedom. Now where do we get the evidence of a human being's freedom? According to Lonergan the most obvious evidence for the freedom of man's decisions lies in the possibility of inconsistency between human knowing and doing. As I mentioned above, one may know what is right but refuse to do it. Therein lies the core of human freedom.

The act of willing, though contingent, is free and systematic. It chooses whatever is grasped by a practical insight. The function of the act of willing is to confer actuality on what it grasps as intelligible after weighing all the evidence presented to it.

Conditions of Effective Freedom

Lonergan puts forward conditions for effective freedom under four headings. These are: external circumstance, the subject as

---

[192] *Insight*, 643.

sensitive, the subject as intelligent, and the subject as antecedently willing.[193] I will present them briefly.

1. External Circumstances: These are whatever external constraints hinder the freedom of human kind. Anything that may offer a limited range of concretely possible alternatives, such as enslavement, is an external circumstance for effective freedom. One may be physically challenged to perform ordinary normal duties. If someone is injured in a car accident and is confined to a wheelchair, for certain this person will not be free to climb a tree. If someone has one hand amputated, he/she may not be effectively free to play the piano.

2. The Subject as Sensitive: These are limitations that arise from one's psycho-neural state. These states need higher integration from intelligence and the will. This situation can be realized especially when one is learning a talent that needs special attention. Take for example, when a person is learning how to play the violin, he/she will not be effectively free until he/she has mastered that skill. It may take some time before he/she develops the habit of playing the violin. Until the time when he/she can comfortably sit and produce a beautiful melody with his/her instrument, he/she cannot be termed to be effectively free.

3. The Subject as Intelligent: These are the limitations of intellectual development. Just examine the struggle involved in the process of learning. Once a person grasps an insight, he/she can repeat it at will. But when he/she has not yet reached that point, the struggle remains and this is a limitation in the effective freedom. The greater a person's accumulation of insights, the broader is the base from which he/she can move towards further insights.

4. The Subject as Antecedently Willing: "Will" is the bare capacity to make decisions. Willingness is the state in which persuasion is not needed to bring one to a decision. Willing, finally, is the act of deciding. Now the function of willingness runs parallel to the function of the habitual accumulation of insights. What one does not understand yet, one can learn; but learning takes time, and until that time is devoted to learning, other possible courses of action

---

[193] *Insight*, 645-47.

are excluded. Similarly, when antecedent willingness is lacking, persuasion can be invoked; but persuasion takes time, and until that time is devoted to persuading oneself or to being persuaded by others, one remains closed to otherwise possible courses of action.[194]

Let us now use an illustration to help understand effective freedom. Jenifer is a clinical officer employed by a certain government who is working in a public hospital. The government orders clinical officers in all public hospitals to administer antifertility drugs to adolescent girls in order to control population growth in that particular country. Jenifer is in a dilemma. On the one hand, her faith does not allow to do what the government is demanding her to do. On the other hand, if she refuses to adhere to the demands of the government, she may lose her job.

Jenifer is essentially free, but apparently not effectively free. Essentially, she is free to adhere to the demands of the government and she really can do so with less effort. But her conscience is dictating something else. Let us now see whether Jenifer is affected by the conditions of effective freedom. Jenifer may fear intimidation from her colleagues and her employer. Her life may also be in danger if she doesn't cooperate with her colleagues in executing the government's orders. Therefore, her freedom is affected by external circumstances. Jenifer also knows clearly that what the government is asking is contrary to her religious beliefs. Her conscience is put to the test. Her psycho-neural demands are now put into confusion. She is not free until her conscience settles the matter. Finally, Jenifer is not willing to join her colleagues in doing what the government is demanding.[195] She is not yet persuaded enough. So, in this case, Jenifer is not effectively free.

Lonergan reminds the reader of one more important point. The process of rational decision making is parallel to the process of knowing. Thus,

---

[194] *Insight*, 646.

[195] Note that if Jenifer will not adhere to the government's demands, she has already made a decision. She has made a decision to obey her conscience. By making this decision, she should be ready to face the possible consequences.

As long as one is moving towards full self-possession, the detached and disinterested desire to know tends to be in control. But once one is in the state of rational self-consciousness, then one's decisions are in control, for they set the objective of one's total activity and select the actions that are to lead to the goal. So it is that a person, caught as it were unawares, may be ready for any scheme or exploit but, on the second thoughts of rational self-consciousness, settles back into the narrow routine defined by his antecedent willingness. For unless one's antecedent willingness has the height and breadth and depth of the unrestricted desire to know, the emergence of rational self-consciousness involves the addition of a restriction upon one's effective freedom.[196]

Finally, Lonergan attests that effective freedom has to be won. And how will this be possible? According to him, the key point is to reach a willingness to persuade oneself and to submit to the persuasion of others. For then one can be persuaded to a universal willingness; one becomes antecedently willing to learn all there is to be learnt about willing and learning and about the enlargement of one's freedom from external constraints and psycho-neural interferences.[197] One needs to remain genuinely open to reflection and to rational persuasion in order to possess effective freedom.

Lonergan's Contribution

1. It is Lonergan who meticulously demonstrates how the pure desire to know grasps intelligently and affirms reasonably, not only the facts of the universe of being, but also its practical possibilities of choosing. The consistency between knowing and doing can be achieved only by a willing will. A conscious effort has to be made by the will for one to be consistent in moral living.

2. The differentiation between essential and effective freedom brings a new and important dimension into the understanding of freedom. This differentiation brings to the surface the fact that human

---

[196] *Insight*, 646.
[197] *Insight*, 646-47.

beings are essentially free agents, but there are some conditions which may prevent these free agents from actualizing their freedom.

3. As agents of free will, we need to keep on evaluating our moral actions. The success of this evaluation will depend on our engagement in self-appropriation. The more genuinely we engage in our self-appropriation, the better the results of our moral choices and decisions.

4. In fact, the essence of freedom is that the will may decline or accept to move itself to its free act.

Concluding Remarks and Suggestions

1. The question of freedom has occupied the minds of philosophers and theologians for centuries. The debate is still ongoing in the contemporary society on delimitations of human free will. We cannot say that we have exhausted all what needs to be said about this important existential topic. What I believe is that we have made some strides in the right direction.

2. Lonergan has given us a method which will help us understand some of those intriguing questions about free will.

3. By nature, as human beings, we are endowed with a lot of freedom, provided we fulfill the existential conditions seen above. However, we should be fully equipped to take full responsibilities of our rational actions.

4. We suggest the following:
   a. We need to engage ourselves in a serious self-appropriation in order to realize our sense of freedom.
   b. We need to go deeper into ourselves and ask those fundamental questions as pertaining our free will. Do we experience a sense of freedom in our rational selves? Do we exercise free will in our choices and decisions?
   c. We too need to ask the question of consistency: do we experience dichotomy in our knowing and doing? Does our free will always follow free action?

Having discussed the question of moral freedom and responsibility, the next chapter remind us that in our free choices, there is always a high possibility of making wrong choices because of the interference of bias.

Case Study 6: Free will vs Duty

An ethical moral dilemma may arise in situations where the moral and religious beliefs of health workers interfere with the duty of health care professionals to provide optimal service to clients and to "do no harm."

Janet is a health worker. Her client wants her to perform an abortion, but this action is contrary to her religious beliefs. Jane follows her conscience and refuses to perform an abortion on her client. Jane's action is based on her contention that to do so would violate her religious beliefs. Her client goes into depression and anxiety, and decides to go to court to sue Jane for violating her basic freedom of choice. The law of this particular country permits procuring of an abortion. Jane is convicted, and she has to serve six years in jail.

Questions for Deliberation

1. In what ways is moral consistency evident in the case of the health worker, Jane?
2. Do you think that health workers should decline to provide services to those individuals whose lifestyle they find morally wrong?
3. In what ways was Jane's decision morally justifiable?
4. Did Jane act out of her free will, and was her free will violated?

VII. The Four-fold Bias

To err is human, and common sense is very human. Besides the bias of the dramatic subject, of the individual egoist, of the member of a given class or nation, there is a further bias to which all men are prone. For men are rational animals, but a full development of their animality is both more common and more rapid than a full development of their intelligence and reasonableness.[198]

Questions for Reflection

1. What do you understand by "bias"?
2. Have you ever felt biased in any situation?
3. Do you think biases can lead to inconsistences?
4. Are you able to recognize bias in yourself?
5. Are you able to recognize bias in others?

Introduction

Lonergan presents four types of bias in chapters 6 and 7 of *Insight*. These are dramatic, individual, group and general bias. The first bias is treated in chapter 6 while the rest are found in chapter 7 of *Insight*. It is interesting to note that the four biasare treated in the two chapters of *Insight* with the title *"common sense."* Biases are found in all classes of people. Joseph Flanagan refers to biases as 'conscious dialectical tensions operating in each person.'[199] In

---

[198] *Insight*, 250.

[199] Joseph Flanagan, *Quest for Self-Knowledge: An Essay in Lonergan's Philosophy*, (Toronto: Toronto University Press, 1997) 79. Cited hereafter as Flanagan, *Self-Knowledge*.

chapter two, we saw how insights emerge. Biases are flight from insight. We also saw that one can consciously or unconsciously prevent insight from emerging. Lonergan ventured to show how the four different but related dialectical tensions unfold and thereby set the conditions for four different ways by which knowers may prevent insights from emerging. Unfortunately, biases hinder the full development of human understanding.

Dramatic Bias

The first type of bias to be treated by Lonergan is dramatic bias. It appears in chapter six of *Insight*, just after the discussion on the dramatic pattern of experience. In the dramatic pattern of experience, Lonergan articulates the artistic drama of life in which the human person is involved. This drama starts from birth, continues through interaction with others till the end of a person's life. It is in the drama of life that a person accumulates knowledge by learning from his/her own experiences and from the community he/she is living in. In the drama of life, the characters are molded by the drama itself. Insights emerge and accumulate in this drama of life. Lonergan observes that,

> *As other insights emerge and accumulate, so too do the insights that govern the imaginative projects of dramatic living. As other insights are corrected through the trial and error that give rise to further questions and yield still further complementary insights, so too does each individual discover and develop the possible roles he might play, and under the pressure of artistic and affective criteria, work out his own selection and adaptation.*[200]

In the dramatic pattern of experience, as Lonergan has revealed above, ordinarily insights are desired and are acquired. But we find this is not always the case. Insights can be unwanted. Lonergan explains what exactly it means to refuse an insight. He believes that "to exclude an insight is also to exclude the further questions that would arise from it, and the complementary insights that would carry

---

[200] *Insight*, 211-12.

it towards a rounded and balanced viewpoint."[201] Dramatic bias prevents a person from engaging in asking further questions which would generate further answers for the accumulation of knowledge. It is a disastrous bias not only for our private lives, but also for our social living. It can lead to misunderstanding both in ourselves and in other people. We are not able to have a balanced outlook on life. Now there is an imminent danger which is brought by the dramatic bias. When misunderstanding escalates, and we are unable to understand ourselves and others, the result is withdrawal from the outer drama of life and entry into the inner drama of fantasy.[202] There is a split between the persona that appears in public and the private inner ego. If this situation is not taken care of in time, we may feel unwanted and eventually enter into depression. Let us now look into the psychic elements of dramatic bias.

Scotosis

Lonergan calls such an aberration of understanding a scotosis.[203] Fundamentally, a scotosis is a disease of the preconscious censorship, and is therefore unconscious. However, it also emerges into consciousness in various ways. Unwanted questions, images, and insights may emerge in a random way. If they do so, they are handled in a variety of ways: by suppressing further questions, by rejecting the insights as mere bright ideas, or by rationalizing the scotosis. Thus, the scotosis remains fundamentally unconscious, and yet the mind is troubled, bewildered, and oscillates between suspicion and reassurance.

Repression[204]

While scotosis does emerge into consciousness in some way, we have explained that it is basically a disease of the preconscious censorship. Normally the censorship encourages the emergence of schematic images which will give rise to an insight. When an insight

---

[201] *Insight*, 212.
[202] *Insight*, 212.
[203] *Insight*, 215.
[204] *Insight*, 215-16.

is unwanted however, it has the opposite effect of repressing from consciousness any scheme that would suggest the insight.

Normally, the censorship is constructive; it arranges materials that emerge into consciousness in a perspective helpful to insight. Naturally, this also implies that other materials are left behind. However, this does not involve the introduction of any patterns into this material. In scotosis however, the primary activity of the censorship is repressive: it facilitates the exclusion of arrangements into the unconscious. Schemes that would lead to the unwanted insight are positively excluded; all other materials are allowed to emerge.

Thus, repression is a basically preconscious activity; it must be distinguished from conscious refusal to behave in a particular fashion (sometimes also referred to as 'repression'). We restrict the name 'repression' "to the exercise of the aberrant censorship that is engaged in preventing insight."[205]

Inhibition[206]

Repression leads to an inhibition of neural demand functions. Now neural demand functions may be demands for images or demands for affects. Both are not inhibited in the same fashion, for insights arise from images and not from affects, and so what is to be repressed are images, while affects will be repressed only if connected with unwanted images. What sometimes happens is that affects get dislodged from images, and attach themselves to some other associated but 'unproblematic' images. This can give rise to strange behavior: sexual arousal occasioned by unlikely images, or emotional upsets caused by harmless things.

---

[205] *Insight*, 216.
[206] *Insight*, 216-17.

Dreams[207]

The peculiarity of dreams is that this experience is not dominated by a pattern, and the censorship is relaxed. Because of this, neural demands not met during the day become active. Dreams are a way of giving expression to unsatisfied neural demands, and they are a means of restoring equilibrium. Therefore, they function as a safety-valve.

Since there is no dominant pattern in dreams, and since space and time are also loosened up, affects and images may often be found in strange combinations, leading to incongruous dreams. There is however no reason to be shocked by such dreams: they are expressions of neural demands which have been excluded from waking consciousness by the conscious and responsible performer; they are not to be taken as representative of that performer.

On the social level also, there is the equivalent of dreams, with a similar function: myths, art, theater, ritual. Random mistakes and adverse situations can be offset by dreams, a healthy environment, adequate instruction and timely guidance, and inner acceptance. However, there can be a chain of such mistakes and situations, and this can lead in time to scotosis. Then the proper development of affective attitudes is hindered, neural demand functions are loaded with inhibitions, affective demands are shifted to incongruous objects. Eventually the conscious dramatic pattern can no longer integrate and give adequate representation to the distorted demand functions. Then neural demands assert themselves in waking consciousness in a variety of ways (the psychoneuroses), and a person loses control over his/her life.

Individual Bias

In his treatment of this bias in chapter 7 of *Insight*, Lonergan starts by clarifying the meaning of the terms, "egoism" and "altruism." There are some characteristics of animal behaviour which cannot be termed "egoistic" such as when they kill their prey to satisfy their biological needs for survival. They do so by following

---

[207] *Insight*, 218.

their natural instincts. Likewise, when an animal takes care of its offspring, we cannot conclude that it is doing so because it is altruistic. It is only following its natural instinctual feelings. This spontaneous behaviour in animals cannot be said to be either egoistic or altruistic. It is just their ordinary way of responding to their biological instinctual calling. Lonergan observes this spontaneity of animals and concludes that it is possible to find a similar attitude in human beings as they interact in their social lives. He believes that in some instances, "men are led by their intersubjectivity both to satisfy their own appetites and to help others in the attainment of their satisfactions; but neither type of activity is necessarily either egoistic or altruistic."[208] Lonergan goes further to clarify what he means by "egoism". According to him, "egoism is neither mere spontaneity nor pure intelligence but an interference of spontaneity with the development of intelligence…Egoism, then, is an incomplete development of intelligence."[209] Egoists are not unintelligent. They can think for themselves. In a very shrewd way, they can solve their problems diligently. But unfortunately, they refuse to raise further relevant questions which are necessary for the progress in knowledge. They don't allow complete free play to intelligent inquiry. In the natural set up, egoists would continue repeating the same old wisdom proverbs without using their own personal intelligence to interpret them.

Lonergan defines "common sense" as specialization of intelligence in the particular and the concrete.[210] This definition is very important if we want to understand how egoists operate. Usually, egoists operate in the realm of common sense. Their intelligence is specialized in particular instances. They try to apply their inherited wisdom to particular issues without necessarily asking further questions. They may need an addition of an insight to solve a particular issue in a particular situation. What happens is that, once that situation has passed, the added insight is no longer relevant, and so the common sense of an egoist may immediately revert to its

---

[208] *Insight*, 244.
[209] *Insight*, 245.
[210] *Insight*, 198-99

normal state of incompleteness.[211] Therefore, egoists lack sufficient understanding. For their liberation, they need to realize their insufficiency and then to raise further relevant questions which may lead to the accumulation of insights. This is the only way which can lead to the further development of their personal intelligence.

Finally, Lonergan believes that egoists are not totally unaware of their self-deception. Their conscience keeps on disturbing them. They are aware of the criterion used by philosophers in reaching the truth. They are aware that there is a process of raising further relevant questions for the accumulation of insights. Their conscience keeps on reminding them of their sin against the light. As Lonergan observes this is manifest in the egoist when "operative within him there is the eros of the mind, the desire and drive to understand; he knows its value, for he gives it free rein where his own interests are concerned; yet he also repudiates its mastery, for he will not grant serious consideration to its further relevant questions."[212] So if an egoist knows the value of the desire and drive to understand (and especially when it comes to his/her issues), then he/she should liberate him/herself, come out of his/her 'cave' and enjoy the light and warmth of the pure desire to know.

Group Bias

The third type of bias to be treated by Lonergan is what he called "group bias". He contrasts it with individual bias. He explains that, "while individual bias has to overcome normal intersubjective feeling, group bias finds itself supported by such feeling. Again, while individual bias leads to attitudes that conflict with ordinary common sense, group bias operates in the very genesis of common sense views."[213] This indicates that group bias, since it is supported by intersubjective feeling, could be even more disastrous than individual bias in the development of societies.

---

[211] *Insight*, 199.
[212] *Insight*, 247.
[213] *Insight*, 247.

In ordinary living, we have social stratification. Take for example in any company, there is a hierarchy of employees. We find owners, chief executive officers, managers, directors, secretaries, and workers in various departments. These groups of persons are defined implicitly by the pattern of relationships of a social order in that particular company. For a company to be successful, and to ensure its effective progress in making profit, each group has to perform its tasks well and equally support other groups. The top management has to make sure that the human resource management is well coordinated, that it creates confidence and sentiments of trust among everyone in the company, and that there are cordial and mutual relationships among the different groups. This example can be applied in any social groups. However, positive mutual relationships are not always possible. What is sometimes observed is an individual group's selfish interests. Lonergan argues that,

> *this formation of social groups, specifically adapted to the smooth attainment of social ends, merely tends to replace one inertial force with another. Human sensitivity is not human intelligence, and if sensitivity can be adapted to implement easily and readily one set of intelligent dictates, it has to undergo a fresh adaptation before it will cease resisting a second set of more intelligent dictates.*[214]

Now, how does social progress come about if there is unhealthy competition among the groups? We are aware that progress is brought about by the noble ideas of great minds. Each new idea that is brought forward is supposed to gradually modify the social situation and call for further ideas which bring about further modification. But now there is a problem. Lonergan keenly observes that groups are made up of individuals who are not "pure intelligences". The new ideas are practical and they are applied to real concrete situations. The problem is that "while the practical common sense of a community may be a single whole, its parts reside separately in the minds of members of social groups, and its development occurs as each group intelligently responds to the

---

[214] *Insight*, 248.

succession of situations with which it immediately deals."[215] This human situation prevents continuous progress of institutions or societies. Group spontaneity may not accept all the changes and thus it may prevent further development. Just as we saw how the egoist prevents further insight from occurring, so too the group spontaneity may prevent further relevant questions arising thus prohibiting further development of society. Simply put, we talk of group bias when we find a kind of "refuge" (in the sense that whatever he/she thinks, does or says, is highly influenced by that particular class/group) in a certain group, a certain race, a certain nation, a certain class, a certain club, a certain society, a certain tribe etc.

General Bias

Besides dramatic bias, individual bias and group bias, there is another type of bias which all human beings are in danger from. It is what Lonergan calls "general bias". It was Aristotle who said that men are rational beings. But is the rationality of human beings always in the forefront of their activity? Lonergan acknowledges that "men are rational animals, but a full development of their animality is both more common and more rapid than a full development of their intelligence and reasonableness."[216]

Men and women have been gradually moving towards a better understanding of the dialectical tensions working in them. Humanity has already made some strides. History shows that our intelligence has played a vital role in shaping who we are. We have seen that human beings are not pure intelligences. It takes considerable training to remain in the purely intellectual pattern of experience. Other native desires seem even stronger in us and may take control of most of our time. Most people find themselves more comfortable in common sense living. And sometimes "common sense people" tend to ridicule any form of abstraction. We have seen the limitations of common sense. It specializes in the concrete and the particular. It is not able to define its terms. Every specialized field (and person) is prone to the general bias of common sense. Specialists should be

---

[215] *Insight*, 248.
[216] *Insight*, 250.

open to recognize and appreciate experts in other fields and be able to work together with them in mutual collaboration, in this way expanding each other's horizons.

The Longer Cycle of Decline

There is another unfortunate situation. Lonergan observes that the general bias of common sense can combine with the group bias and cause more harm to the progress of a society. We can think of how difficult it is to correct the distorted ideas of religious, social and political groups. The origins of the longer cycle of decline originate in the general bias of common sense. What does this mean? Lonergan explains that "the longer cycle is characterized by the neglect of ideas to which all groups are rendered indifferent by the general bias of common sense."[217] To understand what Lonergan means by "longer cycle of decline", Flanagan has written:

> *To grasp the results of this long cycle of decline, let us recall that the basic dialectic is between the interested, practical knowing of common sense and the disinterested desire of theoretical knowing. While there is a tension and opposition between these two concrete conscious poles, there could be harmonious complementarity. But for such complementarity to emerge, people who are working out day-to-day solutions to the problems of practical living must realize that common sense is a specialized pattern of knowing that is limited to particular problems and particular solutions. It cannot deal adequately with problems inherited from past generations that are blocking questions, insights, and ideas that could become operative if these inherited biases and disorienting cultural assumptions were recognized and removed. In other words, common-sense knowers must realize and acknowledge their own limitations and agree to cooperate with knowers whose insights and ideas have*

---

[217] *Insight*, 252.

their source, not in short-term objectives and practices, but in long-term concerns and consequences.[218]

It now becomes clear that the main problem is brought about by the dialectic of knowing and in the method of solving issues in the realm of practical common sense and in the realm of theoretical science. Is there a solution to this problem? What is needed to reverse this general bias is a new and higher viewpoint that will attack the problem at its source. Flanagan puts it correctly when he comments: "What is needed is a method that can interpret the historical sequence of cultures in a critically normative way. The purpose of such a critique would be, not just to understand human history, but to understand it in a way that human communities can become more responsible for the history they have inherited and for the history they are making and transmitting to further generations."[219]

Lonergan's Contribution

1. The four biases had been present and operating in each one of us prior to their formulation and presentation by Lonergan. But it is Lonergan who shows clearly and distinctly how they operate and affect us.

2. It is Lonergan who stresses that just as insights can be desired, so they can also be unwanted. This is the power of dramatic bias actively acting within us, preventing us from making progress in our quest for knowledge. This decline eventually leads us to disregard all the transcendental precepts.

3. Lonergan reminds us that we are all born with a strong egoistic tendency. If this tendency is not tamed early on, it can degenerate and prevent us from further progress in self-transcendence. It may prevent us from reaching out to others in altruism.

4. It was Aristotle who was the first to acknowledge that man is a social being. Lonergan analyses the dynamic of living together

---

[218] Flanagan, *Self-Knowledge*, 86-7.
[219] Flanagan, *Self-Knowledge*, 88.

which can result in either progress or decline depending on the absence or presence of group bias. Group bias can be so devastating that it excludes from our presence all those who do not 'belong to us.'

5. Finally, Lonergan identifies another kind of bias from which it may not be so easy for us to escape. This is what he calls general bias. He seems to be saying that this is in our genetic make-up. The fact is that our irrationality seems to be more developed than our rationality. It seems easier for us to adopt the irrational behavior of moral decadency than to be more rational and humane in our moral behavior.

Concluding Remarks and Suggestions

1. Biases are part and parcel of our ordinary lives. It is almost impossible to live in an environment which is completely devoid of biases. It is also a big challenge for each one of us to eliminate completely the biases in us.

2. The elimination of biases is a lifelong task, and sometimes it can be a slow process that demands endurance. Even though it is a lifelong process, the good news is that after recognizing our biases, there is the possibility of recovery.

3. Biases are found in the four patterns of our experience: the biological, aesthetic, dramatic and intellectual.

4. Biases are the source of alienation and if not attended to, can cause serious and devastating decline in both an individual's and a community's progress.

5. For this reason, we suggest the following:

    a. In every moment of learning, let us try to identify the possible biases which we could be carrying in our baggage.

    b. After identifying any possible biases, let us take courage and seek the means of eliminating them.

c. Let us be ready to undergo a process of conversion. (Details for this process will be discussed in the next chapter).

Lonergan will lead us through the journey of conversion in chapter eight.

Case Study 7: Legislators

In a certain parliamentary assembly, the debate went on for hours. The ethos of the parliament was rather rough. Members of the assembly could not agree on any of the issues that were brought forward for discussion. The debate went on late into the night and the members began asking why they had not been successful in getting a single motion passed that day. It later emerged that a certain group of legislators had vowed to block any measure put forward by another group of lawmakers who came from a seemingly insignificant party.

1. Can you recognize bias in the lawmakers?
2. What kind of bias or biases are evident in this case?
3. In this situation, what do you think is the remedy?

VIII. A Call to Conversion

As orientation is, so to speak, the direction of development, so conversion is a change of direction and, indeed, a change for the better. One frees oneself from the unauthentic. One grows in authenticity. Harmful, dangerous, misleading satisfactions are dropped. Fears of discomfort, pain, privation have less power to deflect one from one's course. Values are apprehended where before they were overlooked. Scales of preference shift. Errors, rationalizations, ideologies fall and shatter to leave one open to things as they are and to man as he should be.[220]

Questions for Reflection
1. What do you understand by "conversion"?
2. Have you ever experienced "conversion" in your life?
3. Are you able to distinguish intellectual conversion from other types of conversion?
4. Do you think conversion is necessary to attain moral consistency?

Introduction

We have discussed the four biases as presented by Lonergan in the sixth and seventh chapters of *Insight*. We have seen how these biases can distort our way of knowing being, our way of reaching objectivity, our way of making rational moral decisions and our way of being in love with the transcendent. They are responsible for a real distortion of our intellectual, religious and moral development. In the

---
[220] *Method*, 52.

present chapter, we shall examine the possibility of eliminating these biases through the process of conversion. It is important to note that Lonergan does not use the term "conversion" in the most familiar sense (such as being converted to join a certain religious group). In the words of Patrick Byrne: "conversion in the more fundamental sense begins with an act of choice. It is a decision to follow the lead of the transcendental notion of value and being-in-love in an unrestricted fashion."[221]

I will not give the historical background of Lonergan's threefold conversion that starts much before *Insight*. Instead, I will begin with his thought in *Method in Theology* in which he identifies three kinds of conversion: intellectual, religious and moral. Robert M. Doran identified a fourth type that he termed, "psychic conversion,"[222] which Lonergan also acknowledged. However, I will not explore this fourth type of conversion. Those who would like to know more about psychic conversion, should consult Doran's *Subject and Psyche.*[223]

Before discussing "conversions," Lonergan gives the context in which they exist. And he starts by showing the real source of conflicts.

Conflicts

It is important to note that Lonergan deals with the topic of 'conversion' in the fourth functional specialty, Dialectic, in *Method in Theology*. Dialectic deals with conflicts. According to Lonergan, the cause of conflicts may lie in religious sources, in religious tradition, in the pronouncements of authorities, or in the writing of theologians.[224] Sources of conflict may be found in more contexts than Lonergan lists, but the context in which Lonergan is writing is a theological and philosophical context.

---

[221] Byrne, *Discernment*, 225.
[222] Robert M. Doran, *Theology and the Dialectics of History* (Toronto: University of Toronto Press, 2001), 42-63.
[223] Robert M. Doran, *Subject and Psyche*, (Milwaukee: Marquette University Press, 1994).
[224] *Method*, 235.

Conflicts occur due to contrary opinions we have in various fields of expertise. Lonergan points out that there are some fundamental conflicts which stem from explicit cognitional theory, an ethical stance, or a religious outlook.[225] The conflicts which stem from this reality (of the three mentioned above) are more profound and may be more difficult to resolve because they modify an individual's mindset. These conflicts call for intellectual, moral and religious conversion. Lonergan gives a method to engage in resolving these conflicts – the dialectic. In his own words, "dialectic will be able to bring such conflicts to light, and to provide a technique that objectifies subjective differences and promotes conversion."[226]

Horizons

We know very well the literal meaning of the word "horizon." When I was a little child, I used to think the earth and the sky embraced each other at some distant point. This was my understanding of horizon at that time. It was the limit of my field of vision. But I came to realize that as I moved towards that vantage point, it always seemed to move ahead of me. Then I could not understand why the vantage point seemed to move ahead of me. It was only later, after attending some geography classes, that I came to understand the meaning of "vantage point." Lonergan explains that "for different standpoints, there are different horizons. Moreover, for each different standpoint horizon, there are different divisions of the totality of visible objects."[227] We come from different cultural backgrounds. Our educational backgrounds differ according to the country or continent we come from. We belong to different religious affiliations. Our political and social viewpoints are quite divergent. All these differences remind us that our outlook on reality differs greatly.

Our outlook on life will differ. The scope of our knowledge and the range of our interests vary according to with the period in which we are living, our social background and milieu, our education and

---

[225] *Method*, 235.
[226] *Method*, 235.
[227] *Method*, 235-6.

personal development. Every day is an opportunity to expand our horizons. Think, for example, what happens to us when we learn a new language? We open ourselves up the possibility of speaking to and understanding millions of other people who speak that particular language. Our boundaries and limits are widened. Our horizons are widened. Something similar happens to the person who opts for conversion.

Conversions

In trying to make a distinction between a horizontal and vertical exercise of freedom Lonergan borrows a statement from Joseph de Finance. de Finance explains that "a horizontal exercise is a decision or choice that occurs within an established horizon. A vertical exercise is the set of judgments and decisions by which we move from one horizon to another."[228] These sets of judgements help a person to move from an old to a new horizon which may be deeper and richer than the old one and offer new potentialities. Lonergan notes that it is also possible that the movement to a new horizon will involve an about-face.[229] This may entail a completely new beginning, a new lease of life. Such a new beginning is what Lonergan calls "conversion".

Lonergan gives us three types of conversion: intellectual, religious and moral. He believes that these three conversions are distinct but related to each other. And so, he presents each conversion separately and then ventures to show how they are related to each other. These conversion processes take place in two basic stages: radical conversion and ongoing conversion. In radical conversion, as Tyrell explains, there is a "turning from" a fundamentally destructive form of living and a "turning toward" a constructive, life-creating and fulfilling way of life. Ongoing conversion entails a confirmation of

---

[228] *Method*, 237.
[229] *Method*, 237.

the "turning from," or radical conversion, as a result of which a person demonstrates a rejection of destructive tendencies.[230]

Intellectual Conversion

Lonergan recognizes that the dynamic structure of human knowing and choosing comprises a compound set of operations: experiencing, understanding, and judging. Intellectual conversion is a radical clarification and, consequently, the elimination of an exceedingly stubborn and misleading myth concerning reality, objectivity, and human knowledge.[231] Lonergan wants to put things straight. Every philosopher gives his own version of epistemology, metaphysics and objectivity. In some cases, we have witnessed real conflict such as that between the empiricist and the rationalist in modern philosophy. Lonergan wanted to correct the myth that had been put forward in the history of philosophy. "Knowing" had been portrayed as just looking, "objectivity" as seeing what was there to be seen and not seeing what was not there, and "the real" was what was "out there now" to be looked at. Lonergan called this outright myth. For him, the source of this myth is the lack of distinction between the world of immediacy and the world mediated by meaning. The world of immediacy is the world of sense experience (seeing, hearing, touching, smelling, feeling). But this is not all that is involved in knowing "the real" and reaching "objectivity". Lonergan proceeds to explain what the world mediated by meaning means:

> *Knowing, accordingly, is not just seeing; it is experiencing, understanding, judging, and believing. The criteria of objectivity are not just the criteria of ocular vision; they are the compounded criteria of experiencing, of understanding, of judging, and of believing. The reality known is not just looked at; it is*

---

[230] Bernard, Tyrell, "Passages and Conversions." in *Creativity and Method: Essays in Honor of Bernard Lonergan*. Ed. Matthew L. Lamb (Milwaukee: Marquette University Press, 1981), 13.

[231] *Method*, 238.

given in experience, organized and extrapolated by understanding, posited by judgment and belief.[232]

Gregson underlines this fact when he observes that "if knowing is like looking then all one has to do is open one's eyes and one would not only see but know as well. Under the sway of this ocular myth, what is seen becomes the most important reality thereby negating objectivity and promoting subjectivity."[233] For Lonergan, only the critical realist can know clearly the facts of human knowing and pronounce the world mediated by meaning to be the real world. He/she is able to do this only inasmuch as he/she shows that the process of experiencing, understanding, and judging is a process of self-transcendence. In this way, Lonergan introduces a new dimension in knowing reality and reaching objectivity – the process of self-transcendence. Self-transcendence is achieved by a person's moving beyond his/her own selfish pursuit and is realized in every instance of correct understanding, responsible decisions and genuine love. This is the only process which helps a person to transit from the world of immediacy to the world mediated by meaning. Lonergan invites the reader to realize that intellectual conversion is the gateway to further knowledge and development.

Religious Conversion

Religious conversion is being grasped by ultimate concern. It is "otherworldly" falling in love. It is total and permanent self-surrender, without conditions, qualifications, reservations.[234] This entails a radical change in a person. According to Lonergan, religious conversion is interpreted differently in the context of different religious traditions. "For Christians it is God's love flooding our hearts through the Holy Spirit given to us. It is the gift of grace, and since the days of Augustine, a distinction has been drawn between

---

[232] *Method*, 238.

[233] Gregson, V., "The Desire to Know: Intellectual Conversion." in *The Desires of the Human Heart: an Introduction to the Theology of Bernard Lonergan*, (New York: Paulist Press, 1988), 26.

[234] *Method*, 240.

operative and cooperative grace."[235] Lonergan points out that the human capacity for self-transcendence becomes achievement when one falls in love. It is not ordinary "falling in love" as happens when a person falls in love with another human being, but falling in love with the transcendent necessary Being. This love of God changes our entire existence. This unrestricted love is the heartbeat of a genuine religion. It sets a new horizon, resets our values and alters our knowing. We need to realize that religious conversion is a gift. And this gift is freely given to the hearts of those who cooperate with the giver.

Lonergan distinguishes two types of graces – operative and cooperative. Operative grace is the replacement of the heart of stone with a heart of flesh, a replacement beyond the horizon of the heart of stone. Cooperative grace is the heart of flesh becoming effective in good works through human freedom. Operative grace is religious conversion. Cooperative grace is the effectiveness of conversion, the gradual movement towards a full and complete transformation of the whole of a person's living and feeling, his/her thoughts, words, deeds, and omissions.[236] Just as with intellectual and moral conversion, religious conversion too calls for self-transcendence.

Moral Conversion

Patrick Byrne observes that what Lonergan had to say about moral conversion is less clear than what he said about either intellectual or religious conversion.[237] (For a fuller understanding of the extension of Lonergan's moral conversion, I refer the reader to Byrne's *The Ethics of Discernment*, 227-36).

According to Lonergan, moral conversion changes the criterion of a person's decisions and choices from satisfaction to values.[238] It is true that before we have attained the age of reason, our parents and other mentors persuade us to do what is right. Sometimes we are

---

[235] *Method*, 240.
[236] *Method*, 240.
[237] Byrne, *Discernment*, 227.
[238] *Method*, 240.

actually forced to do what is right and avoid what is wrong. But this is not the case when we mature. On reaching maturity, we are in a position to make independent choices. We decide for ourselves and in so doing we are making ourselves for better or worse, depending on the choices we make. Lonergan invites us to make the exercise of vertical freedom. According to him, moral conversion consists in opting for the truly good, even for value against satisfaction when value and satisfaction conflict.[239] Knowing what is right is not enough. Deciding what to do is still not enough. Doing what is, in fact, right, is the real test of moral conversion. A person may be prevented from acting in a morally right way by the biases which we discussed in chapter 7 above. To grow into moral conversion, a person has to be open to listen to the advice and opinions of others, and able to choose what is truly good. A person must also be ready to accommodate criticism from others concerning his/her moral conduct. Lonergan puts this challenge to his listeners:

> *One has to keep scrutinizing one's intentional responses to values and their implicit scales of preference. One has to listen to criticism and to protest. One has to remain ready to learn from others. For moral knowledge is the proper possession only of morally good men and, until one has merited that title, one has still to advance and to learn.*[240]

Moral conversion is deeper and demands more of us than many of us imagine. Some people may think that they are morally converted if they live "good and holy lives." Others may think that since they don't disturb other people in the community, and because they are seen as exemplary by the majority, then they are morally converted. While still others may think that since they are able to make independent good moral judgments and are able to live in accordance with the precepts of religion and society, they are morally converted. This conception of moral conversion is insufficient. Moral conversion implies embracing every truly good value in the entire ecosystem of the universe. Byrne is correct in stating that:

---

[239] *Method*, 240.
[240] *Method*, 240.

> *one does not become morally converted by focusing exclusively upon the value of the person one is becoming while ignoring what seem to be the unrelated values, for moral conversion is a decision which will culminate in the personal acceptance of all values, including, for example, the value of health and athletic excellence, of virtuoso musical and dramatic performances, of masterpiece of fine art, of great discoveries in science and scholarship. [...] Moral conversion places one's own decisions and other acts in a much larger whole universe of values, replete with its true rankings of value priorities. The questions that set ethical ("real") self-transcendence in motion are questions about true rather than apparent values. Morally converted persons have more and different questions about every potential course of action. Such persons do not ask merely whether this course of action will yield pleasure or even physical well-being. They go on to ask about and consider seriously how it would contribute to the improvement, perseverance, or corruption of their society, their culture, their personhood, or the satisfaction of the world. Such persons ask not merely how a course of action will affect them individually, or even how it will affect their immediate family and friends. They ask with seriousness about the implications for the nature and for human beings distant on the globe and distant in the future. Morally converted ethical questioning challenges satisfaction and complacency, and moves us onwards towards judgments about true values.*[241]

This is a summary of the holistic meaning of moral conversion. It is a highly complex matter which demands personal and collective responsibility. It also demands a lot of self-discipline and good will that help orient an individual towards authenticity. It may take an entire lifetime for those who are really determined to be fully morally

---

[241] Byrne, *Discernment*, 230.

converted. However, every day is an opportunity to take a bold step towards authentic moral conversion.

Lonergan's Contribution

1. Use of the term "conversion" is not new, especially in the religious sphere. The context in which Lonergan uses the term, and brings out the three-fold nature of conversion, is breathtaking. Conversion is the process as a result of which we make a total and radical change (or an about-face) in our lives. It invites us to shed harmful, dangerous, misleading satisfactions and adopt values which will lead to total authenticity.

2. The biases discussed in chapter seven above which distort our way of knowing, choosing and doing are eliminated by this process of conversion.

3. When we are "intellectually" converted, our perception of reality, objectivity, and human knowledge is more authentic.

4. When we are "religiously" converted, our being is grasped by ultimate concern. We surrender ourselves permanently, without conditions, qualifications or reservations to the Supreme Being. It is an 'otherworldly" falling in love.

5. And when we are "morally" converted, we embrace every truly good value in the entire ecosystem of the universe.

Concluding Remarks and Suggestions

1. Conversion brings forth objectification of our horizon. Our horizons become clearer and broader only after attaining a three-fold conversion in the way explained by Lonergan.

2. When we are morally converted, our criteria for making decisions and choices change from mere satisfactions to true values.

3. Let us reflect on the following:

    a. Let each one of us ask ourselves: am I intellectually, morally and religiously converted?

b. Or am I intellectually converted but not morally and religiously converted?
   c. Or am I intellectually and morally converted and not religiously converted?
   d. We need to be honest with ourselves in sincerely answering all the above questions.

Why should we strive for the three-fold conversion? I suggest each one of us needs some fulfilment and happiness in our lives. Chapter nine will discuss the question of happiness.

Case Study 8: Harassment by Senior Officer

A woman is physically and emotionally harassed by her senior manager in a large company. She decides to sue the company, and during settlement discussions, she is offered an extremely large amount of money to settle the case. In return, the woman is required to confirm that the manager did nothing wrong. Before the date scheduled for her to sign the settlement agreement, a criminal investigation agent comes to know about the deal. He is also offered a large amount of cash for his silence. The company wants to keep the senior manager because he is a big money maker for the company.

Questions for Deliberation

1. What are the issues of integrity, ethics and law presented in the case study?
2. What options does the woman have, and what should she do, and why?
3. In this case study who needs "conversion"?
4. Do you find moral inconsistency in the actions of the woman and the criminal investigation agent?

necessary to produce happiness, such as desiring to get rid of bodily pain, or desiring a state of inner tranquility. Only when we are in pain do we feel the need to seek pleasure, a need which inevitably only produces greater pain. In order to get rid of this "pain-pleasure-pain" cycle, we need to cultivate a mindset in which there is no pain. Thus, the aim is not the positive pursuit of pleasure, as it was for Aristippus. The aim is rather the attaining of a neutral state which is best described as "peace of mind."[253] The Greek word Epicurus uses for this state is *ataraxia*, which literally means "freedom from worry."

Epicurus also notes that we need wisdom to see which pleasures are really pleasurable, and which pains are necessary to produce pleasure. Some pleasures lead to greater pain, like imbibing copious amounts of alcohol, and so the wise person will shun them. On the other hand, certain pains, like sadness, can lead to an appreciation for life or to compassion, which are highly pleasurable states. We should not therefore get rid of all negative emotions but only those that lead to unnecessary pain. In keeping with this sentiment, Epicurus disparages the "crass hedonism" which emphasizes physical pleasure; instead, he claims that the philosophical pursuit of wisdom with close friends is the greatest of pleasures. Based on this conception of happiness, it is the philosopher who is the happiest of all people, for he chooses the stable pleasures of knowledge over the temporary and volatile pleasures of the body.[254]

In short, for Epicurus, the purpose of philosophy was to attain a happy, tranquil life, characterized by peace, freedom from fear, the absence of pain, and by living a self-sufficient life surrounded by friends. Epicurus taught positive thinking. A person will be happy in life when he/she has trained themselves to think positively. According to Epicurus, inner happiness comes from inner peace. When a person calms down, inner happiness appears. Epicurus regarded philosophy as medicine for the soul. He defined life's sole good as happiness, which he equated with pleasure. Epicurus was very clear on the highest type of pleasure which gives the highest

---

[253] Epicurus, "Letter to Menoeceus"

[254] Epicurus, "Letter to Menoeceus"

amount of happiness – pleasure of mind. He is of the opinion that everyone should be guided by intelligent decisions based upon logical reasoning.

The Good Flow of Life - Stoicism

The three most significant stoics are Zeno of Citium (c. 300 BC), Cleanthes (331-323 BC), and Chrysippus (c. 280-206 BC). It is believed that Stoic philosophy started with Zeno. He believed that happiness was a "good flow of life". Cleanthes was of the opinion that "living in agreement with nature" brought a "reasonable happiness", while Chrysippus believed it was "living in accordance with experience of what happens in nature"[255] that brings happiness. Stoic ethics is a particularly strong version of eudaimonism. According to the Stoics, virtue is necessary and sufficient for "eudaimonia". The Stoics make a radical claim that the eudemonic life is the morally virtuous life. Moral virtue is good, and moral vice is bad, and everything else, such as health, honour and riches, are merely 'neutral'. The stoics went further in condemning external goods such as wealth and physical beauty as not good at all. For them, moral virtue is both necessary and sufficient for "eudaimonia". This Stoic doctrine re-emerges later in the history of ethical philosophy in the writings of Immanuel Kant, who argues that the possession of a "good will" is the only unconditional good.

God as the Highest Good - St. Thomas Aquinas
(1225–1274)

Already in his *Summa Contra Gentiles*, Aquinas had taken a position similar to St. Augustine's, that perfect happiness is not possible in this lifetime. This world is too plagued with unsatisfied desires for anyone to achieve that ultimate good which we all seek by nature. Furthermore, God has basically created us with a desire to come to perfect knowledge of Him, but this is hidden from us while we are in our mortal bodies. True knowledge of God requires our

---

[255] Baltzly, Dirk, "Stoicism", *The Stanford Encyclopedia of Philosophy* (Spring 2019 Edition), Edward N. Zalta (ed.), https://plato.stanford.edu/archives/spr2019/entries/stoicism/

being able to see him directly, but this is only possible for a completely purified soul.

The Thomistic ethical theory differs fundamentally from that of St. Augustine. Its fundamental premise states that God created everything for a purpose. According to Aquinas, the goal of every creature is to seek what is good for itself and inasmuch as man's highest good is God, his ultimate objective must be to attain the *vision of God,* an accomplishment only partially attainable in this earthly life, but perfectly attainable in the life to come.[256] Aquinas believes that one can attain true understanding and communion with God by becoming like him as much as possible. He calls this the state of blessedness or grace and argues that it is a state of supreme happiness resulting from the fullest possible realization of man's true self.[257] In agreement with Aristotle, St. Thomas claimed that the contemplative life is the highest and best life that there is, the most blessed and happiest.[258] Aquinas is uncompromising in his view that our true happiness can only be found in knowledge of God. No other worldly good or pleasure can truly provide us with the ultimate good we seek.

The Intellectual Love of God as the Highest Happiness - Rene Descartes (1596 – 1650)

He is regarded as the father of modern philosophy and the initiator of continental rationalism. As a rationalist, he held that truth is derived from reason and that reason is superior to sense experience. In his book *Passions of the Soul*, Descartes presented an ethical theory which includes Aristotelian elements. He listed six fundamental emotions (admiration, love, hate, desire, joy and sadness) from which all other passions are derived. He held that the most perfect or highest emotion is the intellectual love of God, that

---

[256] Thomas Aquinas, *Summa Theologica,* 1a. lxxxviii. 3, ad 1. Cited hereafter as *Aquinas, Summa Theologica.*

[257] Aquinas, *Summa Theologica,* 1a-2ae. i, Prologue

[258] Aquinas, *III Contra Gentes* 34.

happiness arises from consciousness of perfection and that we are virtuous insofar as our reason remains in control of our passions.[259]

Happiness as "True Pleasure" - John Locke (1632-1704)

According to Locke there is an important distinction between "true pleasures" and "false pleasures." False pleasures are those that promise immediate gratification but are typically followed by more pain. Locke gives the example of alcohol, which promises short term euphoria but is accompanied by unhealthy side effects on the mind and body. Most people are simply irrational in their pursuit of short-term pleasures, and do not choose those activities which would really give them more lasting satisfaction. Thus, Locke is led to make a distinction between "imaginary" and "real" happiness.

However, Locke's moral theory is also "eudemonic", in that it is founded on the presumption that people will pursue their own happiness. Its difference to Epicurus' theory is that Locke insists on grounding morality in divine command. In his understanding of morality, a person should seek happiness in the next world rather than in this one.[260] According to Locke, worldly happiness is an insufficient foundation for any morality.

Utilitarianism as the Greatest Happiness - Jeremy Bentham (1748 – 1832)

Jeremy Bentham was the founder of classical utilitarianism. The greatest happiness for the greatest number (greatest-happiness-principle) is the guiding principle of Bentham's ethics. An act is therefore morally right if it is good for many people. For Bentham, the quantity of happiness is the deciding factor. He identified "utility" as the greatest happiness principle, that is, as the means to achieve

---

[259] Rene Descartes, *Passions of the Soul* (Indiana: Hackett Publishing Company, n.d.) 44. Cf. also Sahakian, *History of Philosophy*. 134.

[260] Greg Foster, *John Locke's Politics of Moral Consensus*, (Cambridge: Cambridge University Press, 2005) 185. Cited Hereafter as Foster, *John Locke's Moral*

"the greatest happiness of the highest number."[261] For him, universal happiness is the common good. In order to determine which of alternative actions is to be preferred, he devised the famous hedonistic calculus.

Self-actualization as the Highest Happiness - Abraham Maslow (1908 – 1970)

Abraham Maslow is a modern psychologist specializing in the study of human behavior. He is one of the first psychologists to focus attention on "happy individuals" and their psychological trajectory. He is most well-known for his "hierarchy of needs."

Inspired by the work of the humanistic psychologist Erich Fromm, Maslow insists that the urge for self-actualization is deeply entrenched in the human psyche, but only surfaces once the more basic needs are fulfilled. Once the powerful needs for food, security, love, and self-esteem are satisfied, a deep desire for creative expression and self-actualization rises to the surface. Through his "hierarchy of needs," Maslow succeeds in combining the insights of earlier psychologists such as Freud and Skinner, who focused on the more basic human instincts, and the more upbeat work of Jung and Fromm, who insisted that the desire for happiness is equally worthy of attention.

Abraham Maslow essentially made self-fulfillment and happiness a central part of his life's work. In a break from the other experts of his time, he wanted to understand what motivated the great people of history and to understand human potential; he wanted to know what humans are capable of as their "healthiest self".

The top pier of Abraham Maslow's hierarchy is dubbed "self-actualization." Maslow studied happy people in order to determine what it was that made them happy or, self-actualized. He refers to "peak experiences" as the experience of happiness. He notes that self-actualized people tend to experience a steadier, more grounded sense of well-being and satisfaction with life. According to Maslow, self-

---

[261] Jeremy Bentham, *An Odyssey of Ideas*, ed. Mary P. Mack, (London: Heineman Publishers, 1962) 106-7. See also Sahakian, *History of Philosophy*. 216.

actualizing people perceive reality accurately; they have a sense of awe, wonder, and gratitude about life. They are not self-centered but rather problem-centered and focus on how to improve things and consequently are not deficiency-centered. They are independent thinkers and are not overly influenced by the general culture. Their sense of humor is not sarcastic or hurtful but rather "life-affirming", in fact, it is a philosophical sense of humor.

"The Good" for the Highest Happiness: Lonergan (1904 – 1984)

In the *Symposium* Plato identified "the good" closely with "the beautiful". He is of the opinion that "the good" is in things by themselves. He calls the *form of the good* "the brightest region of being." He concluded that "the good" is the basis of this orderly universe. In his *Summa Theologica*, St. Thomas identifies virtue with "the good." In his conception of morality, Kant conceives free will as directed towards "the good" of the other. We saw earlier that the Golden Rule also seeks "the good" of the other.

In the first place we want to acknowledge that the above different usages of the term "the good" may not necessarily be analogous. Secondly, we have identified the fact that all the meanings attached to the term, "the good", are positive, and are directed towards something of great benefit to the well-being of humanity. From this understanding, we can infer that the teleological objective of "the good" is to provide happiness to humanity. Lonergan does not tell us what "the good" is, but he tells us how to approximate the "the good."

The Notion of the Good

In chapter 12 of *Insight*, Lonergan gives a second order definition of "being". By giving a second order definition, Lonergan wants to remind us that the human mind cannot define "being" as such. "Being" is the totality of reality, and so to define "being" as such, one needs to understand everything about everything. This is impossible. And so Lonergan offers a second order definition that defines being not on the basis of what being is, but on how we can know being. Thus, he says, "Being, then, is the objective of the pure desire to know. By the desire to know is meant the dynamic orientation manifested in questions for intelligence and for reflection."[262] From this second order definition of being, Lonergan affirmed that the intelligibility of being follow spontaneously from whatever is grasped intelligently and affirmed reasonably. The notion of being is closely related to the notion of "the good".

Now, how do we come to understand "the good"? "The good" too, cannot be defined directly. It can only be defined at a second remove. Patrick Byrne explains correctly that "human beings could only define "the good' if they already knew everything good about every good thing… [and he continues to give a second order definition of the good]. "The good" is the objective of the unrestricted notion of value. "The good" is what is to be known in the totality of answers to the totality of questions of value."[263] So to understand what "the good" means, we have to ask appropriate questions of value.

Lonergan argues that "the goodness of being comes to light only by considering the extension of intellectual activity that we name deliberation and decision, choice and will."[264] We have already discussed this intelligibility of being explicitly in chapter two, and implicitly in other chapters. We have given a second order definition of being. We have shown how this "being" is to be known. In this chapter, we are focused on the intelligibility of 'the good.' Lonergan extends the intellectual activity to the activities of deliberation, decision, choice and will. We will start by presenting the levels of "the good".

Levels of the Good

Lonergan presents the first level of the good as the elementary level. He states categorically that on this level, "the good is the object of desire, and when it is attained it is experienced as pleasant,

---

[262] *Insight*, 372.
[263] Patrick H. Byrne, *The Ethics of Discernment: Lonergan's Foundations for Ethics*, (Toronto: University of Toronto Press, 2017) 311. Cited hereafter as Byrne, *Discernment*.
[264] *Insight*, 619.

enjoyable, satisfying."[265] It is true that we all desire 'the good.' We desire good food. We desire a good picnic. We desire good people. We desire good education. Most of the things we desire are in the biological, dramatic and esthetic patterns of experience. These are necessary things for enhancing our physical/biological lives. These objects of our desire are on the plain level of experience. These things can either be tasted, touched, smelt, felt or seen. Without these objects of desire, we cannot truly exist. We need them for our survival. It is common knowledge that when we eat good food, or when we have a good swim, or after a good picnic we generally 'feel good'. Our physical bodies respond well when they are treated well. On the other hand, what happens when we lack 'good things' in our daily encounters? When our bodies are not treated well, we start feeling sick, we start feeling pain, we start feeling "bad". The experience of pleasure is no longer with us. This is the experience on the first level of 'the good'. On this level we can experience only individual "goods" which anticipate satisfactions or dissatisfactions.

But the desires are not all on the same level. There is a desire which is unique. This is the detached, disinterested, unrestricted desire to know.[266] We have already discussed this type of desire in chapter two. This desire manifests itself in the intellectual pattern of experience. Just like any other desire, it has its satisfaction. It goes beyond mere satisfactions. According to Lonergan, this desire "of itself, heads beyond one's own joy in one's own insight to the further question whether one's own insight is correct. It is a desire to know, and its immanent criterion is the attainment of an unconditioned that, by the fact that it is unconditioned, is independent of the individual's likes and dislikes, of his wishful and his anxious thinking."[267] Do human beings desire to know, and not only just to know, but to know correctly? Does our knowing reach the unconditioned, which is detached from our likes and dislikes? Are our judgments free from our wishful thinking? This desire to know is a desire but at a higher level which leads to a higher good.

---

[265] *Insight*, 619.
[266] *Insight*, 619.
[267] *Insight*, 619.

THE NOTION OF HAPPINESS

Lonergan goes ahead to discuss the second meaning of the good.

> *Besides the good that is simply object of desire, there is the good of order. Such is the polity, the economy, the family as an institution. It is not the object of any single desire, for it stands to single desires as system to systematized, as universal condition to particulars that are conditioned, as scheme of recurrence that supervenes upon the materials of desires and the efforts to meet them and, at the price of limited restrictions, through the fertility of intelligent control, secures an otherwise unattainable abundance of satisfactions.*[268]

We are moving from the level of individual human goods to the level of the social good. The polity, the economy and the family are all institution which produce social good. These institutions strive for "the good of order". "This good of order" is realized in systems. Lonergan contends that this good is identified as the dynamic order of proportionate being. We see economies growing. Their dynamics of operating keep on changing. We see politics changing every day. New parties appear and new manifestos are drawn up from time to time. We see new orientations for the families. They develop, sensitive to the signs of the times. They are systems on the move. These systems, to some extent, keep balance with the dynamic unfolding of the individual desires and aversions.

The good of order possesses its own normative[269] line of development, inasmuch as elements of the idea of order are grasped by insight into concrete situations, are formulated in proposals, are accepted by explicit or tacit agreements, and are put into execution only to change the situation and give rise to still further insights.[270] The good of order stimulates subjects to raise further questions. It is

---

[268] *Insight*, 619-20.

[269] Normative generally means relating to an evaluative standard. Normativity is the phenomenon in human societies of designating some actions or outcomes as good or desirable or permissible and others as bad or undesirable or impermissible. A normative statement expresses a value judgment about whether a situation is desirable or undesirable.

[270] *Insight*, 620.

in the raising of the questions that the institutions are formed, that parties are constituted, that ideologies such as socialism, capitalism and communism emerge. These are possible constructions of human intelligence and possible systems for ordering the satisfaction of human desires. Still, we find that people are free to embrace certain systems and reject others.

In any social development, two factors have to be considered: the dynamic material to be ordered and the subjective conditions under which the order is discovered, communicated, accepted, and executed.[271] The subjective conditions involve the human psyche which is subject to either individual, group or general biases. When these biases interfere with the general ethos of the society, decline can result; hence, the good of order is required to prevent further decline. The events in the natural settings of social institutions which bring about the social good of order may follow schemes of recurrence. The good of order is also necessary for the amendments which could have been caused by the deviators of the society and initiate the process of attaining once again the progress.

Now we move to the third level of the good which we call "value". In the first level we saw the good of desire manifests itself in ordinary living as pleasant, enjoyable, and satisfying. In the second level, the good of order manifests itself not as the object of any single human desire, but as universal condition to particulars that are conditioned. Now the third type of good which is linked to the good of order, emerges on the level of reflection and judgment, of deliberation and choice.[272] Lonergan reminds us that human intelligence is not only speculative, but also practical. After the insight grasps the sufficiency of the evidence, it issues a speculative judgment of fact. But human intelligence is not yet satisfied with this judgment of fact. It moves further to meet the question of value. Is it worthwhile? Is it worth accepting or rejecting? These are the questions of practical intelligence. They are the questions for deliberation. Now one may ask: how do we come to grasp "the good" as value? According to Lonergan, "it is in rational, moral self-

---

[271] *Insight*, 620.
[272] *Insight*, 620.

consciousness that the good as value comes to light, for the value is the good as the possible object of rational choice. Just as the objects of desire fall under schemes of recurrence to give rise to the good of order grasped by intelligence, so also the good of order with its concrete contents is a possible object of rational choice and so a value."[273] Let us now look into the ontology of the good.

The Ontology of the Good

We have been concerned with the good in the human sense. We have seen that the good is the object of desire, the object of the intelligible orders and also as the object of value. This reveals to us how ethics is so much related to metaphysics. Lonergan generalizes this notion to conceive the good as identical with the intelligibility that is intrinsic to being.[274] He puts forward the idea of potential, formal and actual good. He identifies potential good with potential intelligibility which includes and extends beyond the order of desire. Then he identifies formal good with formal intelligibility which includes but also extends beyond human intelligible orders. Finally, he identifies actual good with actual intelligibility which includes and extends beyond human values.[275] We may ask why Lonergan identifies every instance of proportionate being with the three basic elements (potency, form, act) which correspond to the three basic cognitional acts (experience, understanding and judging). According to Byrne,

> *his [Lonergan's] identification of the three components of any proportionate good is the fundamental basis for his distinction between value and the good. Values and actual goods are one kind of good, but not the only kind. Particular and potential goods, goods of order and formal goods and their various constituents, are also good. But none of these alone is the whole of the good. Likewise, values, by themselves, are not the whole of the good. It is true that the transcendental notion of value*

---

[273] *Insight*, 624.

[274] *Insight*, 628.

[275] *Insight*, 628.

> *ultimately intends goodness in the fullest sense, and that this is the whole of all values and actual goods. Still, by intending that whole, the notion of value also intends all the components that are related to and indispensable to actual goods/values. So the components of the potential and formal good also are good. Still, their goodness is distinguishable from the goodness of value.*[276]

Lonergan notes that the three levels of the good take place in the concrete universe of the proportionate being.

We need to revisit how we reach the point where we are compelled to make a rational judgment of fact. We normally allow the act of reflective understanding to complete the whole process of examining the data; then again, the reflective understanding has to meet the question for reflection by transforming the prospective judgment from the status of a conditioned to the status of a virtually unconditioned. Lonergan observes that the "rational self-consciousness cannot consistently choose the conditioned and reject the condition, choose the part and reject the whole, choose the consequent and reject the antecedent. Accordingly, since man is involved in choosing, and since every consistent choice, at least implicitly, is a choice of universal order, the realization of universal order is a true value."[277]

Lonergan brings the point home. He leads the reader to realize that the individual human goods participate in the wholeness of the universal order, and consequently to realize that universal order is to realize a true value. The realization of universal order is the realization of all existents and all events (environmental concerns). This points to the transcendental notion of value which Byrne has hinted at above. Byrne argues that Lonergan's argument can be extended still further, leading to the affirmation of the goodness of the whole being without restriction – transcendent being as well as proportionate being.[278] It is not the intention of this chapter to discuss

---

[276] Byrne, *Discernment*, 364.
[277] *Insight*, 628-9.
[278] Byrne, *Discernment*, 370. See also *Insight*, 663.

this notion of the transcendent being. This aspect will be our point of focus in the next chapter of the question of God.

Lonergan's Contribution

1. In this chapter, we have presented the notion of happiness as discussed and explained by various philosophers. Lonergan's approach is quite different. He explains 'how' to reach the genuine happiness by approximating the question of "the good".

2. Genuine happiness is reached by choosing 'the good.' This good is presented in the three levels, the good of desire, the good of order and the good as value.

3. Lonergan makes it clear that our human intelligence is not satisfied with the speculative judgment of fact. It wants to explore the question of value. Is it worthwhile? Is it worth accepting or rejecting? These are the questions of practical intelligence. Human intelligence is not at peace (happy) until it squarely confronts these questions for deliberation.

Concluding Remarks and Suggestions

1. There is no common definition of "happiness", yet people purport to know what it means. Several meanings have been attached to this term. Most philosophers tend to believe that the "pleasure of the mind" is more intense (and may last longer) than other types of pleasures. Some theologians may not agree with this opinion.

2. Happiness seems to be an important value. Anything which would hinder the attainment of real happiness (or that which would bring some pain) is rejected by most of the people.

3. It is logical to conclude that one of the major objectives of morality is to create happiness or a certain satisfaction in individual persons and societies.

4. We make the following suggestions:
   a. Let us take time and strive to understand the true meaning of happiness.

b. Let us take time and investigate in our social milieu the real sources of true happiness.
c. Let us strive to know the true human good that will lead us to true happiness.
d. Perhaps we could also try to be more altruistic in our living. Perhaps this would open some more avenues for true happiness.

We find that human beings crave for more happiness. Is there teleological dimension to this craving for happiness? Could there be a being who is the source of ultimate happiness? Examining this question is the subject of the last chapter of this book, the question of God.

Case Study 9: Unfulfilled life of Malaren

Malaren is a New Zealand woman who went to the best private schools, both primary and high school in her own country. After attaining a very high grade in high school, she studied at a renowned university in the United States of America. She performed very well at the university and managed to attain the best grade in her class. This made her very popular. On her return to New Zealand, she secured a job at one of the best paying companies. After a few years working, she decided to marry a very wealthy man. She had a very lavish life style. Unfortunately, only later did she come to know that she had blood cancer. Her doctor informed her that her life was coming to an end. She was only 32 years. Malaren had to accept the reality of death at this early age. On her deathbed, everyone was shocked to hear what she said. She called her mother and in a low voice, she whispered, "Mum, I'm dying, but I'm sorry to say that I have lived a lavish and meaningless life. I wish you had been present in my life."

Questions for Deliberation

1. What do you think made Malaren utter those strong words to her mother?

THE NOTION OF HAPPINESS

2. Do you think Malaren could have done something to have lived a better life?
3. Could Malaren' mother have contributed to the sadness in her daughter's life?
4. Do you think that riches are a great source of happiness?
5. Do you think Malaren was morally consistent in the lavish way she lived her short life?

X. The Question of God

Our knowledge of being is by intelligent grasp and reasonable affirmation. By asking what being is, we have been led to grasp and conceive what God is. Since it has been shown that being is the core of all meaning, it follows that our grasp and conception of the notion of God is the most meaningful of all possible objects of our thought. Still, every object of thought raises a further question; for once the activity of intelligent consciousness is completed, the activity of reflective consciousness begins. Is God then merely an object of thought? Or is God real? Is he an object of reasonable affirmation? Does he exist?[279]

Questions for Reflection

1. What is your experience of God?
2. Does the question of God matter to you?
3. Does God have any influence in your decision making?
4. Does the problem of evil in the world disturb you?

Introduction

According to Lonergan, grasping and conception of the notion of God is the most meaningful of all possible objects of our thought. That which is most meaningful then ought to be sought with ultimate care and precision. And we start with the most basic question: is the human intellect capable of intelligently grasping the reality of God? If this is possible, to what extent can it grasp that reality? In this

---

[279] *Insight*: 692.

chapter, we shall present the traditional arguments for 'proving' the existence of God. We shall start with a short African religious experience and the question of God. Then we shall present the *a priori* argument of St. Anselm and then turn to the *a posteriori* arguments or rather the five ways of St. Thomas. After this, we shall explore Lonergan's view on the question of God. Finally we shall turn to the moral question. Is our moral striving basically cognate or alien to the universe? Is the universe itself a value, the result of a value judgment? If it is not, then are we the first originators of value?

African Religious Experience and the Question of God

Introduction

Africa is the world's second largest and second most populous continent; Asia being the largest and most populous. Africa consists about 30.3 million square kilometers including adjacent islands. It covers 6% of earth's total surface area, and 20% of its land area. The most astonishing thing is that, even with the figures above, little is known worldwide about the wealth and potential of Africa. It has a very rich history in all spheres of life: cultural, socio-economic, and religious. We shall take a quick look at the African religious experience and the question of God.

The Experience of God in the African Traditional Religion

It was John S. Mbiti, a renowned Anglican theologian, who, in the introduction of his book *African Religions and Philosophy*, contended that Africans are notoriously religious. Though this contention may not be very accurate in contemporary African society, it is still applicable to many African societies. Although waves of exploration, modernization and globalization have had their impact on the traditional African way of life, religion still plays a very vital role in the daily lives of most contemporary African people. A good number of African people continue to live under the spiritual influence of their ancestral way of life. Probably, the reason for this phenomenon is, as Mbiti puts it, that "Religion is the strongest element in traditional background, and exerts probably the greatest influence upon the thinking and living of the people concerned."[280] A person cannot detach her/himself from the religion of her/his group, for to do so is to be cut off from her/his roots, her/his foundation, her/his context of security, her/his kinships and the entire group of those who make her/him aware of her/his own existence.[281]

Mbiti's main preoccupation was to show that the knowledge and the worship of God were intrinsic part of African life right from the earliest times of their existence on the African continent. He endeavors to show that the sense of God was not something alien to Africans and that it was not introduced by the missionaries who brought Christianity to the continent. Mbiti's work brings to the surface that the God of Christianity was not essentially different from the God the Africans believed in. This is the position taken by many other African scholars including Edward Blyden, and Bolaji Idowu.

The Question of God in the African Context

Like the early Greek cosmologists, the Africans observed the wonder of the universe – all that exists, the trees of the dense forests, the mountains, the rivers, the lakes, the animals, and finally concluded that there must be a being (greater than human beings) that created or put in place, all that. According to Mbiti, in addition to visible things, there is a mystical order of the universe. Africans believed in the existence of invisible, hidden, spiritual power in the universe. They were baffled by the order and came to believe that it cannot originate from itself or from human beings. Therefore, Africans concluded that it originated from God who must be all powerful. Moreover, since no human being was able to explain about the origin of all these objects (visible and invisible) of the universe, they concluded that God must exist.

The question of the existence of God is insignificant in the African Traditional Religions, but the disturbing question is that of his *real* nature. The emphasis is on 'real nature'. This is because some attributes of God were mentioned by many African Traditional

---

[280] John S. Mbiti, *African Religions and Philosophy*, (New York: Doubleday & Company, Inc., 1969), 1. Cited hereafter as *Mbiti ARP*.

[281] Mbiti *ARP*, 3. Addition of female gender case is author's.

Religions such as all-powerful, ever-present creator, supreme being etc. This reveals that they had some idea of the nature of God. Traditional African religions believed that a powerful God exists, but did not know fully the nature of this existence. Does he have a body like human beings? Which language does he speak? Does he have a community? Does he get hungry and tired like human beings? These were the disturbing questions about the nature of God in the African Traditional Religions. However, there seems to be no written argumentations in the African Traditional Religions to prove the existence and nature of God.

Common Traits in African Traditional Religion

It is true that African Traditional Religions are many and differ significantly from one to another. However, there are common traits in all of them. These traits serve to show that Africans had an idea of the nature of God. Aloysius M. Lugira[282] identified six of them listed below:

1. All things in the universe are part of a whole. There is no sharp distinction between the sacred and the non-sacred (or profane).

2. In most African traditions, there is a Supreme Being: a creator, sustainer, provider, and controller of all creation.

3. Serving with the creator are a variety of lesser and intermediary gods and guardian spirits. These lesser gods are constantly involved in human affairs. People communicate with these gods through rituals, sacrifices, and prayers.

4. The human condition is imperfect and always will be. Sickness, suffering, and death are all fundamental parts of life. Suffering is caused by sins and misdeeds that offend the gods and ancestors, or by being out of harmony with society.

5. Ritual actions may relieve the problems and sufferings of human life, either by satisfying the offended gods or by resolving

---

[282] Aloysius M. Lugira, *African Tradition Religion*, Joanne O'Brien and Martin Palmer eds., (New York: Chelsea House Publishers, 2009), 15. Some modifications have been done by the author of the current work.

social conflicts. Rituals help to restore in people the traditional values and renew their commitment to a spiritual life.

6. Human society is communal. Ancestors, the living, the living-dead, and those yet to be born are all important parts of the community. The relationships between the worldly and the otherworldly help to guide and balance the lives of the community. Humans need to interact with the spirit world, which is all around them.

One of the most distinctive differences between African Traditional Religions and the most important world religions is that in former, there are no books of reference. There are neither 'holy books' (as the Bible and the Quran) nor written creeds. Cultural beliefs and rules for daily living are written in the hearts of the people and passed on by the word of mouth from one generation to the next.

Ontological Arguments for the Existence of God

Ontological arguments are arguments leading to the conclusion that God exists, drawn from premises which are supposed to derive from some source other than observation of the world, that is, from reason alone. In other words, ontological arguments are arguments from what are typically alleged to be just analytical, *a priori* and necessary premises leading the conclusion that God exists.[283] They are widely considered to be the more fascinating arguments for the existence of an omnipotent and an all-perfect God. While there are several different versions of the arguments, all purport to show that it is self-contradictory to deny that there exists a greatest possible being. Thus, according to this general line of argument, it is a necessary truth that such a being exists; and this being is what believers call God.

The first ontological argument in the Western Christian tradition was proposed by St. Anselm of Canterbury in his famous *Proslogium, 'Discourse on the Existence of God'* in which he defines

---

[283] *The Stanford Encyclopedia of Philosophy*, s.v.v. "Ontological Arguments", accessed on 24th February 2021. https://plato.stanford.edu/archives/spr2020/entries/ontological-arguments/

God as "a being than which no greater can be conceived." He argues that such a being must exist in the mind, even in the mind of the person who denies the existence of God.[284] From this formulation, he contends that if the greatest possible being exists in the mind, it must also exist in reality, for if it existed only in the mind, then an even greater being must be possible – one who exists both in the mind and in reality. Therefore, he concludes, this greatest possible being must exist necessarily in reality. According to St. Anselm, this is a self-evident truth which is undeniable and indubitable. He put his opponents who denied this truth in an awkward position by saying that even 'the fool' can understand this concept, and that this understanding itself means that the being must exist in the mind.

The argument has been summarized accurately by Kenneth Einar Himma in standard form as follows:[285]

1. It is a conceptual truth (that is, true by definition) that God is a being than which none greater can be imagined (that is, the greatest possible being that can be imagined).

2. God exists as an idea in the mind.

3. A being that exists as an idea in the mind and in reality is, other things being equal, greater than a being that exists only as an idea in the mind.

4. Thus, if God exists only as an idea in the mind, then we can imagine something that is greater than God (that is, a greatest possible being that does exist).

5. But we cannot imagine something that is greater than God (for it would be a contradiction to suppose that we can imagine a being greater than the greatest possible being that can be imagined.)

6. Therefore, God exists.

This ontological argument of Anselm generated much interest and discussion in Western philosophy. Nearly all the great minds of

---

[284] *The Stanford Encyclopedia of Philosophy*, s.vv "Ontological Arguments" accessed on 21 May 2020.

[285] Kenneth Einar Himma, "Anselm: Ontological Argument for God's Existence" in the Internet Encyclopedia of Philosophy. https://iep.utm.edu/ont-arg/

Western philosophy had something to say in relation to this argument. René Descartes, the father of modern philosophy, employed a similar argument to Anselm's. He wrote several variations of his argument, and their common denominator was the idea that God's existence is immediately inferable from a "clear and distinct" idea of a supremely perfect being. Two other continental rationalists, Benedict Spinoza and Gottfried Leibniz followed Descartes' way of thinking about God. Spinoza argued that our ideas do not come from ourselves but must come from an external superior cause. Leibniz amplified Descartes' ideas in an attempt to prove that a "supremely perfect" being is a coherent concept. Another, not so well known thinker, Norman Malcolm, revived the ontological argument in 1960 and came out with what is believed to be stronger ontological argument in Anselm's work (we shall see it shortly here below). Emmanuel Kant, although he later criticized the ontological argument, saw the sense in Anselm's argument. He argued that everything that it is possible may exist, and that there must be grounds for this possibility. He thus concluded that every possibility must be based upon a single necessity, which he identified as being God.

Malcom's Modal Version of the Anselm's Ontological Argument

In 1960, Malcolm wrote a paper entitled "Anselm's Ontological Arguments" in which he argues that Anselm gave two related ontological proofs for the existence of God. According to Malcolm, Anselm's key premise in the first argument in Proslogion 2 is that something is more perfect if it exists than if it does not exist. His second argument is a modal argument in Proslogion 3. This is the argument which Malcolm revises and defends.

The central idea here is that though existence is not a perfection, the logical impossibility of nonexistence, that is, necessary existence, *is* a perfection. Lacewing[286] gives a good

---
[286] Michael Lacewing, "Malcolm's Ontological Argument," in *Philosophy for AS.* (London: Routledge, 2014) 190-93.

summary of Malcolm's modal argument for God's existence as follows:

1. Either God exists or does not exist.
2. God can neither come into existence nor go out of existence.
3. If God exists, then He cannot cease to exist.
4. Therefore, if God exists, He exists necessarily.
5. If God does not exist, then He cannot come into existence.
6. Therefore, if God does not exist, His existence is impossible.
7. Therefore, God's existence is either necessary or impossible.
8. However, God's existence is only impossible if the concept of God is self-contradictory.
9. The concept of God is not self-contradictory.
10. Therefore, God's existence is not impossible.
11. Therefore, reasoning from 7 and 10, God's existence is necessary.

This argument did not go unchallenged. One objection is that though it has been argued that the concept of God is self-contradictory, Malcolm simply assumes that premise 9 is true. Another problem is that even if one grants that necessary existence is a property, Malcolm's argument only shows that *if* God exists, then God exists necessarily. Finally, is it true that necessary existence is a perfection? If "x necessarily exists" means "x exists in all possible worlds," why should God's necessary existence across all possible worlds make God greater in the actual world? For in *this* actual world, a necessarily existing God is no greater than a God that contingently exists in this world.[287]

Criticisms and Objections of Ontological Argument

It is a fact that the ontological argument of Anselm received great praise and popularity especially during the Middle Ages. At the same time, it was not well received by some thinkers of Anselm's time and thereafter. Let us look at some of these criticisms.

---

[287] Richard McDonough, "Malcolm's Modal Version of the Ontological Argument" in *Internet Encyclopedia of Philosophy*. https://iep.utm.edu/malcolm/

1. Gaunilo: The first criticism of Anselm's ontological argument came from his contemporary, Gaunilo of Marmoutiers. He invited his reader to conceive an island "more excellent" than any other island. He suggested that, according to Anselm's proof, this island must necessarily exist, as an island that exists would be more excellent.[288] It is possible to see that Gaunilo's criticism does not explicitly demonstrate a flaw in Anselm's argument. It rather demonstrates that if Anselm's argument is sound, so are many other arguments using the same logic, which cannot be accepted.

Anselm responded to Gaunilo's criticism by arguing that his argument applied only to concepts with necessary existence. He suggested that only a being with necessary existence can fulfill the remit of "that than which nothing greater can be conceived". Furthermore, a contingent object, such as an island, could always be improved on, and thus could never reach a state of perfection. For that reason, Anselm dismissed any argument that did not relate to a being with necessary existence.[289]

2. Thomas Aquinas: While proposing his "five ways" in *Summa Theologica*, St. Thomas Aquinas opposed the ontological argument of St. Anselm. He argued that people cannot know the nature of God, and therefore cannot understand God in the way St. Anselm had suggested. According to Aquinas, only God can completely know his essence, and only He could use the argument perfectly.[290] The rejection of Anselm's argument by Aquinas was a big blow because many other Catholic theologians were also to reject his argument.

3. David Hume: According to Scottish empiricist philosopher David Hume, nothing can be proven to exist using only *a priori* reasoning. The argument of Hume goes like this: whatever a person conceives as existent, he can also conceive as non-existent. There is no being, therefore, whose non-existence implies a contradiction. Consequently, there is no being, whose existence is demonstrable. Hume was convinced that a person can have no abstract idea of

---

[288] Cornman, James W. Lehrer, *Philosophical Problems and Arguments: An Introduction* (Hackett Publishing, 1992) 254 - 56.

[289] James W.; Lehrer, Keith, *Philosophical Problems and Arguments: An Introduction* (Hackett Publishing, 1992) 254–256.

[290] *Summa Theologica* Ia. Q2.A1.

existence and therefore he cannot claim that the idea of God implies his existence. The reason behind Hume's argument is understandable because he was a strong empiricist.

4. Emmanuel Kant: Kant's criticism of the ontological argument is found in his *Critique of Pure Reason*. Kant was primarily attacking the rationalists Leibniz and Descates in their support for the ontological argument. Kant questions the intelligibility of the concept of a necessary being. He considers examples of necessary propositions, such as "a triangle has three angles", (which is a tautology) and rejects the transfer of this logic to the existence of God. The necessary proposition, he argues, does not make the existence of a triangle necessary. Thus, he argues that, if the proposition "X exists" is posited, it would follow that, *if* X exists, it exists necessarily; this does not mean that X exists in reality.[291] Kant further argues that since we cannot know God through sense experience, and that since he is outside the realm of experience and nature, (*phenomena*) we cannot know him. This God belongs to the realm of unknowable (*numena*) and therefore the human mind cannot know him. Let us now look into the five ways of St. Thomas Aquinas which are *a posteriori* in nature.

The Five Ways of St. Thomas Aquinas

The five ways (*quinque viae* in Latin), sometimes known as the "five proofs" are, in the philosophical arena, the five logical arguments for the existence of God. They were summarized by the 13th century philosopher and theologian, St. Thomas Aquinas, a Dominican priest, in his *magnum opus*, the *Summa Theologica*. They are: the argument from the "first mover", the argument from causation, the argument from contingency, the argument from degree and the argument from the final cause or ends. A short summary of each of these five ways is included for the sake of those who may not be familiar with them. This will be followed by a brief discussion of some modern and contemporary views of the "five ways".

---

[291] *Stanford Encyclopedia of Philosophy*, s.v.v. "Kant's Critique of Metaphysics". *Accessed on 11 January 2021.*

St. Thomas believed that the finite human mind was not capable of knowing God directly since God's existence is not self-evident to human beings. Therefore, he thought of using ways which are more evident to human beings to demonstrate the fact that God exists. It is important to note that all the five ways are considered to be cosmological arguments.[292]

1. The Argument from the "first mover": St. Thomas argued that in the world we can see that at least some things are changing. Whatever is changing is being changed by something else. If that by which it is changing is itself changed, then it too is being changed by something else. But the chain cannot be infinitely long. Therefore, there must be something that causes change without itself changing. This everyone understands to be God.[293]

2. The argument from causation: In the world, we can see that things are caused by something else. But it is not possible for something to be the cause of itself because this would entail that it exists prior to itself, which is a contradiction. If that by which something is caused is *itself* caused, then it too must have a cause. But there cannot be an infinitely long chain of causation, so there must be a cause which is not itself caused by anything further. This everyone understands to be God.

3. The argument from contingency: In the world we see things that are possible to be and possible not to be. In other words, perishable things. But if everything is contingent and thus is capable of going out of existence, then, nothing should exist now. But things clearly do exist now. Therefore, there must be something that is imperishable: a necessary being. This everyone understands to be God.

4. The argument from degree: We see things in the world that vary in their degrees of goodness, truth, nobility, etc. For example,

---

[292] A cosmological argument, in natural theology, is an argument which claims that the existence of God can be inferred from facts concerning causation, explanation, change, motion, contingency, dependency, or finitude with respect to the universe or some totality of objects. See Online Encyclopedia Britannica "Philosophy of Religion" 2018.

[293] *Summa Theologica*, I, Q 2, A 3. Moreover, the other four ways are from the same book and the same chapter.

well-drawn circles are better than poorly drawn circles. Healthy animals are better than sick animals. Moreover, some things are better than others. Since living things are better than non-living things, and animals are better than plants, no one would choose to lose their human senses for the sake enjoying the longevity of a tree. But judging something as being "more" or "less" implies some standard against which that something is being judged. For example, in a room full of people of varying heights, at least one must be the tallest. Therefore, there must be something which is best and most true, and most a being, etc. Aquinas then adds the premise: what is most in a genus is the cause of all else in that genus. From this he deduces that there exists some "most-good" being which causes goodness in everything else, and this everyone understands to be God.[294]

5. Argument from the final cause: We see various non-intelligent objects in the world behaving in regular ways. This cannot be due to chance since then they would not behave with predictable results. So their behavior must be fixed. But it cannot have been fixed by themselves since they are non-intelligent and have no notion of how to fix behavior. Therefore, their behavior must be fixed by something else, and by implication something that must be intelligent. This everyone understands to be God.

Having presented in brief the five ways of St. Thomas Aquinas, we shall now comment on the discussion which followed the formulation of these five ways.

A Short Critique of the "Five Ways"

The first strong philosophical criticism of the cosmological argument (the first three "ways" of St Thomas) emerged in the 18th century from the British empiricist David Hume and the German transcendental idealist, Immanuel Kant.

Hume argued that inductive reasoning and belief in causality cannot be justified rationally. According to Hume, we never actually perceive that one event causes another, but only experience

---

[294] *Summa Theologica*, I, Q 2, A 3.

the "constant conjunction" of events. Hume believed that the problem of induction meant that to draw any causal inferences from past experience, it is necessary to presuppose that the future will resemble the past, a presupposition which cannot itself be grounded in prior experience.[295]

Kant argued that our minds give structure to the raw materials of reality, and that the world is therefore divided into the phenomenal world (the world we experience and know), and the noumenal world (the world as it is "in itself," which we can never know). Since the cosmological arguments reason from what we experience, and hence the phenomenal world, to an inferred cause, and hence the noumenal world, and since the noumenal world lies beyond our knowledge, we can never know what is there. Kant also argued that the concept of a necessary being is incoherent, and that the cosmological argument presupposes its coherence, and hence the arguments fail.[296]

Some Responses in Defense of the "Five Ways"

The 20th-century Catholic priest and philosopher Frederick Copleston[297] devoted much of his work to a modern explication and expansion of Aquinas' arguments. In 1948, he engaged himself in a heated debate (on the question of God) with Bertrand Russell in a BBC radio broadcast.

---

[295] Isaiah, Berlin, *The Root of Romanticism*, (2nd ed.) (Princeton: Princeton University Press, 2013).

[296] Reichenbach, Bruce (2013). *"Cosmological Argument 3.5" The Stanford Encyclopedia of Philosophy.*

[297] Frederick Charles Copleston, SJ, (10 April 1907 – 3 February 1994) was an English Jesuit Catholic priest, philosopher, and historian of philosophy, best known for his influential multi-volume *A History of Philosophy* (1946–75). Copleston achieved a degree of popularity in the media for debating the existence of God with Bertrand Russell in a celebrated 1948 BBC broadcast; the following year he debated logical positivism and the meaningfulness of religious language with his friend the analytic philosopher A.J. Ayer. See John Searle (2003), *Contemporary Philosophy in the United States* in N. Bunnin and E. P. Tsui-James (eds.), *The Blackwell Companion to Philosophy*, 2nd ed., (Blackwell, 2003), 1.

Copleston – Russell Debate

The Copleston - Russell debate was a heated exchange concerning the existence of God between Frederick Copleston and Bertrand Russell in a 1948 BBC radio broadcast. The debate centered on two points: the metaphysical and moral arguments for the existence of God.[298] Copleston's position was that God's existence could be proven philosophically, while Russell argued to the contrary. Russell argued from the agnostic position, though whether he was agnostic or atheist was not clear. He confessed to his fellow philosophers that he was agnostic.

Copleston argued strongly that the existence of God can be proved from contingency, and held that only the existence of God would make sense of man's moral and religious experience. Copleston's augment went like this:

First, the existence of God can be proved philosophically by a metaphysical argument; secondly, it is only the existence of God that will make sense of man's moral and religious experience. [...] As regards the metaphysical argument, we are apparently in agreement that what we call the world consists simply of contingent beings, that is, of beings not one of which can account for its own existence. You say that the series of events needs no explanation: I say that if there were no necessary being, no being which must exist and cannot not-exist, nothing would exist. The infinity of the series of contingent beings, even if proved, would be irrelevant. Something does exist; therefore, there must be something which accounts for this fact, a being which is outside the series of contingent beings. If you had admitted this, we could then have discussed whether that being is personal, good, and so on. [...] the problem of God's existence is an existential problem whereas logical analysis does not deal directly with problems of existence.[299]

In summary, what Copleston wanted to prove is that in order to explain existence, we must come up with a being who contains within itself the reason for its own existence, that is to say, a being which

---

[298] Mike Springer *(14 November 2012). Bertrand Russell and F.C. Copleston Debate the Existence of God, 1948" Open Culture.*

[299] "Transcript of the Russell/Copleston Radio Debate". Philosophy of Religion.

cannot not exist. This means that God cannot be caused, and so he himself must contain everything needed for his own existence. Secondly, Copleston referred to the fact that God is a *necessary* first cause. If God did not exist, nothing else would be able to exist. God is the first cause and without a first cause, there can be no effect.

However, Russell found both arguments unconvincing. He contended that Copleston's argument from contingency is a fallacy, and that there are better explanations for our moral and religious experience. He rejected the need to find an explanation for the universe and the principle of sufficient reason. For Russell, the universe is just there, and that is all. He argued against the idea of everything in the universe being contingent by saying that we have only experienced a small part of the universe, and so have no way of telling whether everything elsewhere is also contingent. He used an analogy, namely, that human beings in the universe are like an ant on the corner of a king-sized bed. The ant cannot see the whole bed – it can only see the relatively small portion of the bed it is standing on. Likewise, human beings can know only a small field of their world in which they find themselves. And so Russell concluded that we cannot say anything with certitude about the universe and God.

At the end of the debate, nothing substantial was agreed. In fact, Russell declared that he was not sure whether what they were debating had any meaning at all. This debate reveals a deep-seated problem. According to Lonergan, it is conversion and not proof which is at the heart of the matter in regard to God problem. In his view, proofs are usually worked out of believers who wish to provide certain grounds in reason for the faith that is in them.[300] That explains why the debate between Russell and Copleston could not yield any fruits.

Response to Victor Stenger and Richard Dawkins

It is unfortunate to see how some distinguished thinkers, ignorant of the philosophical and theological thought of the scholastic era, try to ridicule the reasoning of St. Thomas Aquinas.

---

[300] Bernard Tyrrell, *Bernard Lonergan's Philosophy of God*, (Dublin: Gill and Macmillan, 1974) 118-19. Cited hereafter as Tyrrell, *Philosophy of God.*

One top physicist, Victor Stenger,[301] for instance, wrote a book in 2007 entitled, "*God: The Failed Hypothesis. How Science Shows That God Does Not Exist.*" In this book, Stenger examines most of the claims made for God's existence. He considers the latest Intelligent Design arguments as evidence of God's influence in biology. He looks at human behavior for evidence of immaterial souls and the possible effects of prayer. He discusses the findings of physics and astronomy in weighing the suggestions that the universe is the work of a creator and that humans are God's special creation. After evaluating all the possible scientific evidence, Stenger concludes that beyond a reasonable doubt the universe and life appear exactly as we might expect if there were no God.

If Stenger had had a little patience to inquire from any decently trained philosopher or theologian, with a knowledge of the history of metaphysics, ontology, and modal logic, they could have warned him of the catastrophic category error in the title of his book. His thought reveals a fundamental misunderstanding of both the key words in the title of his book - 'God' and 'science'. Consequently, the book he wrote turned out to be just a long *non sequitur* based on a conceptual confusion and a logical mistake. It's like a mathematics student looking for algebraic solution from the history library. That would be ridiculous.

Another thinker who fell into a similar pit was Richard Dawkins. He devoted several pages of *The God Delusion*[302] to a discussion of the "Five Ways" of Thomas Aquinas. Perhaps if he truly wanted to write an authentic scholarly work, he could have consulted some great scholars of ancient and mediaeval thought, but moved by his own hubris, he did not do this. As a result, he not only mistook the "Five Ways" for Aquinas's comprehensive statement on why we should believe in God, but ended up completely misrepresenting the logic of every single one of the "Ways", and at the most basic level. Not knowing the scholastic distinction between primary and secondary causality, for instance, he imagined that

---

[301] Victor Stenger, God: The Failed Hypothesis: How Science Shows That God Does Not Exist (New York: Prometheus, 2008) 73.

[302] Richard, Dawkins, *The God Delusion* (New York: Houghton Mifflin Harcourt, 2006) 68.

Aquinas's talk of a "first cause" referred to the initial temporal causal agency in a continuous temporal series of discrete causes.

Dawkins thought that Aquinas's logic required the universe to have had a temporal beginning, which Aquinas explicitly and repeatedly makes clear is not the case. He anachronistically mistook Aquinas's argument from universal natural teleology for an argument from apparent "Intelligent Design" in nature. Dawkins seemed to think that Aquinas's proof from universal "motion" concerned only physical movement in space, that is, "local motion," rather than the ontological movement from potency to act. He mistook Aquinas's argument from degrees of transcendental perfection for an argument from degrees of quantitative magnitude, which by definition have no perfect sum.[303] Thanks are due to the theistic scholars who keep on enlightening the minds of the numerous believers. And thanks are due, too, to the atheistic and agnostic scholars, who keep on provoking the minds of theistic scholars to bring out the truth of the reality of God.

Both Dawkins and Stenger failed to realize that the divine is not a datum to be observed by sense or to be uncovered by introspection. Nor will any intelligible unity or relationship verifiable within such data lead us totally beyond such data to God. Precisely because modern science is specialized of man and nature, it cannot include knowledge of God.[304]

Lonergan and Aquinas: A Critique of Aquinas's Method

The five classical ways (the argument from the "first mover", from causation, from contingency, from degree and from the final cause or ends) found in Aquinas's *Summa* have one thing in common. They are essentially "cosmocentric". They are the result of observing the workings of nature; whereas, as Bernard Tyrell observes, the proofs for the existence of God which Lonergan elaborates find their

---

[303] David, Bentley Hart, *The Experience of God: Being, Consciousness, Bliss*, (New Haven and London: Yale University Press, 2013), 22.

[304] *A Second Collection*, 91.

proximate basis in the existential subject's thematisation of his own cognitive experience.[305]

Lonergan makes a deliberate shift from the abstract classicism of Aquinas to a concrete historical-mindedness approach. Aquinas's classicism was appropriate in his time. It was the time when reality was defined by strict adherence to the Aristotelian laws of logic. The main method used to arrive at objective truth, was the 'logical method', which was basically static and abstract in nature. Classical Thomism believed that truth is immutable and that human nature does not change. Lonergan challenges this presupposed *de jure* position with his method of self-appropriation of the subject. His method of self-appropriation tackles the real concrete being in his dynamic existential-historical development. We can deduce that Aquinas did not have that concern for history with which he might have been able serve contemporary humanity.

We shall see in the subsequent subsections the gradual development of Lonergan's approach to the question of God. This was necessitated by his dynamic method, which is sensitive to the signs of the times. This kind of development would not have been possible using the static method of logic employed by the scholastics. The approach in *Insight* is highly philosophical, coupled with lucid argumentations. The search in *Insight* is for complete intelligibility. Later in *Method in Theology,* more attention is given to the way the question arises, to moral deliberations and to the religious motivations for asking it, the *de facto* role of grace.

The Reality of God: Bernard Lonergan

Introduction

Lonergan names two great thinkers who influenced his early thinking – St. Augustine and St. John Henry Newman. In the epilogue to his masterpiece, *Insight*, Lonergan mentions the important personal transformation wrought in him by a decade's apprenticeship dedicated to exploring the thought of St. Thomas Aquinas. He

---

[305] Tyrrell, *Philosophy of God*, 4.

produced two major exegetical studies of Thomas Aquinas, *Grace and Freedom (1940)*, and *Verbum: Word and Idea in Aquinas (1946)*. From the above works, we can comfortably conclude that Lonergan probed deeply into the thought of Aquinas.

In this part, I will present a short discussion of Bernard Lonergan's understanding of the existence and the nature of God as found in chapter 19 of *Insight*. Then I will show how his concept of God gradually developed in *Method in Theology*. It is extremely important at this point to note that Lonergan prefaced his argument with the appealing claim that while arguments for the existence of God are many, *all* such arguments are implicitly included in the general form of his own argument.[306]

The Question of God in Insight

It is important to note that Lonergan has followed a different order from the order of the Aquinas's *Summa*. In *Summa*, Aquinas first proves the existence of God, and then develops the attributes of God. In chapter 19 of *Insight*, Lonergan works his strong hypothesis in ten subtitles, starting from the notion of transcendence, to idea of being, to causality and all through to finally reaching the affirmation of God. It is only after working out the implications of this hypothesis, does he ask whether we can rationally affirm the transcendent Being, God. Therefore, he is working in reverse order to Aquinas, which matches his order of inquiry.

In the introduction of *Insight*, Lonergan clearly states the aim of his work. In his mind, it was clear that the question is not whether knowledge exists, but what precisely is its nature.[307] Therefore, Lonergan spends a good deal of time trying to explicate the meaning of the nature of knowledge. This explains why in chapter 19 of *Insight* the most fundamental question about God is not whether *He exist*, but the *nature* of His existence. Lonergan further insists that his aim is not to set forth a list of the abstract properties of human knowledge but to assist the reader in effecting a personal appropriation of the concrete dynamic structure immanent and

---

[306] *Insight*, 695.

[307] *Insight*, 11.

recurrently operative in his own cognitional activities.[308] This is an invitation to the reader to appropriate the transcendental precepts[309] as suggested by Lonergan, in his *Method in Theology*; to be attentive, intelligent, reasonable and responsible as he/she approaches the question of God. It is not an easy task.

Let us start by looking at the structure of *Insight*. This masterpiece is composed of 20 chapters, distributed over nearly 900 pages. Our main interest is chapter 19, which is second last chapter of the book. Lonergan had already laid the foundation (for chapter 19) in his earlier chapters. His transcendental method considers four questions.[310] First, "what am I doing when I am knowing?" This yields cognitional theory (chapters 1-10). Second, "why is doing that knowing?" This is the epistemological question (chapters 11-13). The first eight chapters explore human understanding, while the other five reveal how correct understanding can be discerned.[311] Third, Lonergan investigates the metaphysical question which asks, "what do I know when I do that?" (chapters 14-17). The last question is methodological which asks, "what/how therefore should we do?" (chapters 18-20, the method in doing ethics and the method in approaching the question of God). There comes an interesting note. The editors of *Insight* tell us that *Insight* was completed in 1953 (and published in 1957), and that by December 1952 the first 13 chapters had already been written in their final form. Twenty years later, Lonergan declared that with chapter 13, the book could end.[312] This makes clear that Lonergan had already laid the solid foundation of chapter 19 in his presentation of cognition theory and epistemology.

In his article "Bernard Lonergan on Affirmation of the Existence of God"[313] Paul Amour brings out clearly the thought of Lonergan on the existence of God. Amour starts his reflection by acknowledging the authority of St. Thomas Aquinas (discussed

---

[308] *Insight*, 11.

[309] *Method* 20, additional words are given by the author of the current work.

[310] *Insight*, 16 -20.

[311] *Insight*, xx.

[312] *Insight*, xx.

[313] Paul Amour, "Bernard Lonergan on Affirmation of the Existence of God" Cited in *Analecta Hermeneutica*, Vol. 2 2010. Cited hereafter as Amour *"Affirmation"*.

above) in his *"five ways"*. He begins by contrasting Lonergan's approach to that of Aquinas. He argues that while each of Aquinas's five ways demonstrate the existence of God merely by reference to some limited aspect of God's being (i.e., God as first mover, as first efficient cause, as necessary being, etc.), Aquinas concluded each demonstration with the logically problematic phrases, "and this everyone understands to be God" or "and this being we call God."[314] According to Amour, that addition to the conclusion effectively places the conclusion in a referential context more extensive than what can be supported on the basis of the premises alone. Aquinas was clearly philosophizing within a theological context.[315]

Lonergan himself acknowledged that his approach may appear "excessively laborious, complex, and difficult," even to those who have studied his book. He wanted not to select the easiest approach to the notion of God, nor to offer the simplest proof of his existence, but to produce a philosophically sound argument by which we may rationally "advance from proportionate to transcendent being."[316] Here we are talking about the progression from a knowledge of the real that is proportionate to the human cognitional operations of experiencing, understanding, and judging (as expressed in chapters 1-13 of *Insight*) to a rational affirmation of an absolutely transcendent reality (chapter 19).

The Meaning of Being

We may start by asking a very fundamental human question. "What is being? "Lonergan gives a second order definition of being in chapter 12 of *Insight*. One might have expected the traditional definition of being just as it was given by various metaphysicians in the history of philosophy. Lonergan defines being as 'the objective of the pure desire to know.'[317] By the desire to know is meant the dynamic orientation (towards being as its object) manifested in questions for intelligence and for reflection. Lonergan further

---

[314] Amour "Affirmation".
[315] Amour "Affirmation".
[316] *Insight*, 705.
[317] *Insight*, 372.

clarifies that this desire is the prior and enveloping drive that carries cognitional process from sense and imagination to understanding, from understanding to judgment, from judgment to the complete context of correct judgments that is named knowledge.[318] Now it is clear that this desire to know is the ground of all human inquiry. It is this desire that motivates all our intelligent and rational operations. This desire moves humans to correctly understand what is actually the case, to know objectively and to know the real. Being is not 'already-out-there-real now' to be grasped intuitively or empirically by our senses, but it is always known by the mediation of insight and posited in judgment. This leads us to affirm the intrinsic intelligibility of being. Ours is a heuristic definition of being. It manifests not what is known, but rather how what is unknown would come to be known. Lonergan acknowledged that since human understanding is always limited, we cannot fully understand what 'being is'. It can be known only partially and incompletely. Therefore, ours is restricted act of understanding.

Affirmation of God in Insight

Lonergan comes to the affirmation of God towards the last part (part 10) of chapter 19 of *Insight*. He argues that our knowledge of being is by intelligent grasp and reasonable affirmation, and that by asking what being is, we have been led to grasp and conceive what God is.[319] In the earlier chapters of *Insight,* Lonergan led the reader to understand that being is the core of all meaning. If that is the case, it follows that our grasp and conception of the notion of God is the most meaningful of all possible objects of our thought.[320] Lonergan returns to the most fundamental questions for reflection about God: Is God merely an object of thought? Or is God real? Is he an object of reasonable affirmation? And does he exist?[321]

Lonergan is aware of the meaning that the existentialists such as Heidegger had ascribed to the being, the *Dasein,* and so this is not

---

[318] *Insight*, 372.

[319] *Insight*, 692.

[320] *Insight*, 692.

[321] *Insight*, 692.

the meaning Lonergan ascribes to the affirmation that 'God exists'. Secondly, Lonergan clarifies that while the existence of any proportionate being and the existence of God are known by rational grasp and reasonable affirmation, they are not the same. The reason for this is that the existence of proportionate being is a contingent being existence while that of a transcendental being is the existence of a self-explanatory necessary being.[322] One further question may arise: Is it possible to grasp what God is? Lonergan answers that our grasp is not an unrestricted act of understanding but a restricted understanding. Therefore, we cannot grasp fully the reality of God. Finally, Lonergan makes a syllogistic formulation of his argument. He believes that the existence of God is known as the conclusion to an argument. And he makes the following general formulation:

If the real is completely intelligible, God exists. But the real is completely intelligible. Therefore, God exists.[323]

This syllogism may lead the reader to conclude that Lonergan has oversimplified the affirmation of God too much. However, before one comes to such a judgement, one should first take a look at the genesis of and the development leading to this conclusion. Lonergan makes this syllogism after thirty-eight pages (*Insight*, 657-95) of tightly parked argumentation. This syllogism will be intelligible to the person who undertakes the laborious task of looking at the gradual development of the argument in these pages. Let us take a look at the syllogism again. The problematic premise (in terms of providing evidence) is the minor premise ('the real is completely intelligible'). This premise rests on the complete identity of the real and being. As the object of the detached, disinterested, unrestricted desire to know (as seen earlier), being must be completely intelligible. Being is completely intelligible because being is known completely only when intelligent questions are raised and answered.

The Question of God in Method

After nearly twenty years, Lonergan in his *Method in Theology* reworked his approach to answering the question of the existence of

---

[322] *Insight*, 692, additional by the author of the current work.
[323] *Insight*, 695.

God. According to Robert M. Doran, the transition to later Lonergan occurs after 1965 work on 'Dimensions of Meaning.'[324] This new approach is attributed to his new understanding of the intentionality of moral consciousness and the dynamics of religious conversion.[325] This dimension of 'religious conversion' is completely absent in chapter 19 of *Insight*. Lonergan did not make any appeal to religious experience in *Insight*. In *Method*, he emphasizes the dynamism of the human spirit as implicitly raising the *question* of God, in several distinct ways, by its orientation to self-transcendence. The question of God in *Method* is tackled in the fourth chapter on religion. Lonergan, in his now mature position, states that "it is the view that man's spirit, his mind and his heart, is an active power, an *eros*, for self-transcendence; consequently, the subject is related intrinsically and, indeed, constitutively to the object towards which it transcends itself; finally, knowledge, morality, and religion are the three distinct phases in which such self-transcendence is realized."[326]

The Foundation of the Question of God

We need to locate the question of God. We need to know its genesis. We need to know its basic foundation. Lonergan distinguishes four forms of the question of God. The basic form of the question of God consists in the questioning of our own questioning. A first form of this questioning relates to our questions for intelligence:[327] This is the question which seeks to understand the reality of God. Who is this being? What is He like? Why should the proportionate being seek Him? What difference does His presence make to contingent beings? These are some of the questions that emerge in the first form of the question of God. Lonergan directs us to where we can find answers to such questions:

> *Answers to such questions are reached when the desire to understand expressed in the question is met by the satisfaction of actually understanding. Still the desire to*

---

[324] Robert M. Doran, *Subject and Psyche*, (Milwaukee Wisconsin: Marquette University Press, 1994), 233. Cited hereafter as "Doran, *Subject*".

[325] Amour "Affirmation".

[326] *Second Collection*, 110-11.

[327] Doran, *Subject*, 69-70.

> *understand is not simply a desire for a subjective satisfaction. It wants more. It wants to understand the persons and things that make up one's milieu and environment. How is it, then, that the subjective satisfaction of an act of understanding can be the revelation of the nature of the persons and things in one's milieu and environment? Obviously, if intelligence can reveal them, they must be intelligible. But how can they be intelligible? Does not the intelligibility of the object presuppose an intelligent ground? Does not an intelligent ground for everything in the universe presuppose the existence of God?*[328]

Apart from the questions for intelligence, that is, questions which seek understanding, there are also questions for reflection. This is the moment when we make an affirmation, is it so? These questions are answered when we reach a virtually unconditioned. This is a conditioned whose conditions happen to be fulfilled. This is the only way for the contingent beings to pass reasonable judgements. Their existence is conditioned. But Lonergan asks, can everything be contingent? Must there not exist a necessary being, whose existence is unconditioned, to account for the existence of the beings whose existence is conditioned?[329] And there arises the second form of the question of God. The first two forms of the question of God seen above (questions arising from questioning our questions for intelligence and our questions for reflection) are metaphysical in nature. However, the human mind is not satisfied with these two types of questions. It goes further. There are other types of questions. These are questions for deliberation. Questioning these questions results in the third form of the question of God. Lonergan puts it correctly.

> *To deliberate about deliberating is to ask whether any deliberating is worth while. Has "worth while" any ultimate meaning? Is moral enterprise consonant with this world? We praise the developing subject ever more*

---

[328] Tyrrell, *Philosophy of God*, 53.
[329] *Method*, 102.

> *capable of attention, insight, reasonableness, responsibility. We praise progress and denounce every manifestation of decline. But is the universe on our side, or are we just gamblers and, if we are gamblers, are we not perhaps fools, individually struggling for authenticity and collectively endeavoring to snatch progress from the ever mounting welter of decline? The questions arise and, clearly, our attitudes and our resoluteness may be profoundly affected by the answers. Does there or does there not necessarily exist a transcendent, intelligent ground of the universe? Is that ground or are we the primary instance of moral consciousness? Are cosmogenesis, biological evolution, historical process basically cognate to us as moral beings or are they indifferent and so alien to us? Such is the question of God.*[330]

Is that the end of the questioning after questioning the question of deliberation? Is the moral being satisfied in searching for answers? The human mind is still disturbed. There is a void which needs to be filled. This is the search for the divine. This leads to what Lonergan calls religious experience. Underneath the many forms of and prior to the many aberrations, some have found that there exists an unrestricted being in love, a mystery of love and awe, a being grasped by ultimate concern, a happiness that has a determinate content but not an intellectually apprehended object. Such people will ask, with whom are we in love? So in the fourth and final manner there arises the question of God.[331]

Doran puts it correctly: the question of God "arises by questioning the pure question that the subject-as-subject *is*. This pure question, as one, unifies the four levels on which the question of God arises and renders the four forms of the question of God cumulative."[332] From this argument, it becomes clear that the basic question itself of God is the fourth question, namely, the religious

---

[330] *Method*, 102-3.

[331] Tyrrell, *Philosophy of God*, 72.

[332] Doran, *Subject*, 73.

experience question. And so for a person to really understand the question of God, he needs to undergo some religious conversion. Religious conversion has already been discussed in chapter "A Call to Conversion".

Morality and the Question of God

Let us ask a very basic question. Is belief in God required for human beings to be good or to live good lives? Some religious thinkers have argued that in a Godless world, we have no grounds for being persons of good will or for doing what is morally required of us. If there is no God, everything becomes futile. There is no legitimate reason for all our moral actions.

Kai Nielsen says that there are fundamental, unresolved questions about the foundations of morality, and attempts, such as those of Mill, Kant, Sidgwick, and Rawls, to lay out a systematic moral philosophy to assess our moral practices and social institutions have not been remarkable for their success.[333] It is now becoming clearer that there is no good ground for claiming that only through belief in God can we attain sufficient moral anchorage to make sense of our existential lives. It has been established that there is some moral understanding that is logically independent of belief in God. Nevertheless, this argument does not in any way belittle the supremacy of the role of God in morality.

Nielsen has demonstrated logically that we have no reason to believe that, in any important sense, morality is dependent on religion. He has shown in a purely logical sense that moral notions cannot simply rest on the doctrinal cosmic claims of religion. It is true that there is no reason to believe that torturing little children would cease to be bad in a godless world. Perhaps it is possible to have moral consistency even without the idea of God.

---

[333] Kai Nielsen, "God and the Basis of Morality" in the *Journal of Religious Ethics*, Vol. 10, No. 2 (Fall, 1982), 335-50.

Without disrespecting Nielsen's logical thought, I would join John Hick[334] in arguing that to develop a fully human and adequate normative ethic one must make it a God-centered ethic. Only a God-centered morality can meet our deepest and most persistent moral demands. We long for a God who can offer us the promise of a blissful everlasting life with him. Unless we can convince ourselves that we are creatures of such a loving Sovereign, our deepest moral hopes will be frustrated. No purely secular ethic can - nor indeed should be able – to offer such a hope. Without God, our lives will be devoid of significance, and without moral sense. And given human beings' nostalgia for the absolute, human life without God would be devoid of all purpose or at least devoid of everything except trivial purposes.

Lonergan refers the notion of value as a transcendental notion just like the notion of being. In his treatment of 'the subject', he says that "as the notion of being is the dynamic principle that keeps us moving towards ever fuller knowledge of being, so the notion of value is the fuller flowering of the same dynamic principle that now keeps us moving towards ever fuller realization of the good, of what is worthwhile."[335] And how do we know that which is good, that which is worthwhile? Lonergan has proposed his method of knowing in self-appropriation in his *Insight*. But still he pushes the question further, "what is it for a man to be good, and is the world and all what it contains good?" Lonergan gives a straight condition that "this question can be answered affirmatively, if and only if one acknowledges God's existence, his omnipotence, and his goodness."[336]

Thus, without a belief in God, there can be no humanly satisfying morality. Morality built upon the foundation of God is a transcendental morality and is more satisfying, more edifying and more meaningful to the subject.

---

[334] Hick, John "Belief and life: the fundamental nature of the Christian ethic." *Encounter* 20/4 (January, 1959): 494-516.

[335] *A Second Collection*, 71.

[336] *A Second Collection*, 74.

Lonergan's Contribution

1. When we talk about the question of God in religious circles, we cannot fail to mention the great contribution of St. Thomas Aquinas. Lonergan was aware of this giant of the scholastic era. It is extremely important to note the personal transformation wrought in Lonergan by a decade's apprenticeship dedicated to exploring the thought of St. Thomas. It was after mastering the thought of Aquinas, and after weighing its pros and cons that Lonergan made a deliberate shift from the abstract classicism of Aquinas to a concrete historical-mindedness approach.

2. Lonergan makes a shift from the static laws of logic to the dynamic self-appropriation method which meets a concrete subject in his/her historical situation. It is in this context that Lonergan tackles the question of God.

3. The proofs for the existence of God which Lonergan elaborates in Chapter 19 of *Insight* find their proximate basis in the existential subject's thematisation of his own cognitive experience.

4. Lonergan laid a very formidable foundation for exploring the question of God in his presentation of cognition theory and epistemology. It is only when we articulate accurately how we come to know and how we reach genuine objectivity that we are able to tackle the question of God.

5. It is Lonergan who argues strongly that proofs are usually worked out by believers who wish to provide certain grounds in reason for the faith that is in them. Therefore, a discussion between a believer and a non-believer about the question of God may be futile.

6. Lonergan proposes that it only in religious experience that the question of God arises. This is an unrestricted "being in love", a mystery of love and awe, a "being grasped by ultimate concern", a happiness that has a determinate content but not an intellectually apprehended object.

7. Finally, Lonergan make it clear that without a belief in God, there can be no humanly satisfying morality. Morality built upon the foundation of God is a transcendental morality and is more satisfying, more edifying and more meaningful to the subject.

Concluding Remarks and Suggestions

1. Religious experience and the question of God in the African context reveal that Africans had a strong believe in God even before the advent of Christianity and Islamic faith in the continent.

2. The *a priori* arguments of St. Anselm and the logical *a posteriori* arguments of St. Thomas Aquinas popularly known as the "five ways" have been challenged by philosophers, theologians and scientists as insufficient [inadequate??] for proving the existence of God.

3. Lonergan handles meticulously the discussion of the question of God, starting by questioning the very question of the idea of God, and then going through rigorous argumentations to the affirmation of God. He lays down a very convincing argument for the existence of God.

4. For Lonergan it became clear that the challenge concerning the 'question of God' is conversion, not the proofs. It is only a "converted" subject who can articulate the question of God.

5. At the same time, we can confidently conclude that without a belief in God, there can be no humanly satisfying morality.

6. We suggest the following:
   a. We need to find "humble time" to explore in depth the question of God, given how complicated the question is.
   b. Perhaps the critics, or rather those who categorically deny the existence of God, need to enter into a genuine dialogue, first with themselves, and secondly with believers.
   c. Perhaps religious conversion is the basic ground for a genuine dialogue. This may look like a tautology, but may not necessarily be so.

Case Study 10: Freud vs Lewis

(Adapted from "The Question of God")
https://www.pbs.org/wgbh/questionofgod/why/index.html

Twenty-four years after Freud's death, on the morning of November 26, 1963, in Oxford, England, a group of friends and family gathered to mourn the death of C.S. Lewis.

A celebrated Oxford don, literary critic, and perhaps the 20th century's most popular proponent of faith based on reason, Lewis won international recognition long before his death in 1963. During World War II, his broadcast talks made his voice second only to Churchill's as the most recognized on the BBC. His books continue to sell prodigiously and his influence continues to grow.

Lewis embraced an atheistic worldview for the first half of his life and used Freud's reasoning to defend his atheism. Lewis later rejected his atheism and became a believer. In his subsequent writings, he provided cogent responses to Freud's arguments against the spiritual worldview. Wherever Freud raises an argument, Lewis attempts to answer it. Their writings possess a striking parallelism. If Freud still serves as a primary spokesman for materialism, Lewis serves as a primary spokesman for the spiritual view that Freud attacked.

Unfortunately, because Lewis followed Freud by a generation, his responses to Freud's arguments were the last written word. Freud never had the chance to rebut Lewis' arguments. Yet if their arguments are placed side by side, a debate emerges as if they were standing on two podiums in a shared room. Both thought carefully about the flaws and alternatives to their position; both considered the other's views. Their arguments can never prove or disprove the existence of God. Their lives, however, offer a sharp commentary on the truth, credibility, and utility of their views.

But are these worldviews merely philosophical speculations with no right or wrong answer? No. One of them begins with the basic premise that God does not exist, the other with the premise that He does. Their views are, therefore, mutually exclusive - if one is right, the other must be wrong. Does it really make any difference to know which one is which? Both Freud and Lewis thought so. They spent a good portion of their lives exploring these issues, repeatedly asking the question "Is this true?"

Freud argues against the existence of God. He points to the problem of suffering and he develops the psychological argument that the whole concept of God is nothing but a projection of a childish wish for parental protection from the vicissitudes and sufferings of human existence. He also argues against the objection of those who hold the spiritual worldview that faith "is of divine origin and was given us as a revelation by a Spirit which the human spirit cannot comprehend." Freud says this "is a clear case of begging the question" and adds this comment: "The actual question raised is whether there is a divine spirit and a revelation by it, and the matter is certainly not decided by saying this question cannot be asked."

Lewis agrees with Freud that this is indeed the most important question. He writes: "Here is a door behind which, according to some people, the secret of the universe is waiting for you. Either that's true or it isn't. If it isn't, then what the door really conceals is simply the greatest fraud...on record." Because so many people embrace Lewis's answer, Lewis is right: if not true, then the spiritual worldview is not only a fraud but also the cruelest hoax ever perpetrated on the human race. And the only alternative is to follow Freud's advice: to grow up and face the harsh reality that we are alone in the universe. Freud says we may find less consolation, but the truth, harsh as it is, will ultimately set us free from false hopes and unrealistic expectations. But if the spiritual worldview is true, then all other truth fades into insignificance. Nothing has more profound and more far-reaching implications for our lives.

Questions for Deliberation
1. What is the difference in the approach of Freud and that of Lewis to the question of God?
2. Who do you think is the more realistic in his approach to the question of God?
5. Do you think their arguments can prove or disprove the existence of God?

General Conclusion

We started this book with a short historical survey of moral consistency and examined how men in different historical epochs have understood morality. There are some thinkers whose ideas have helped us in understanding several of the moral principles which we have discussed in the ten chapters of this book. Some of the chapters used a historical approach. This approach helped us first to understand the issues from their genesis, and secondly, to see how the thinking about them has developed. In the ancient epoch, two thinkers stand out – Plato and Aristotle. In the medieval era, there was St. Thomas Aquinas. In the early modern era, developments came from Descartes, Hume and Immanuel Kant. Finally, in the last hundred years, Bernard Lonergan has been the key figure. We did not limit our study to an exploration of the historical development of moral consistency; we also introduced some contemporary issues and examined how philosophers have engaged with them.

To summarize: in chapter one we defined the meaning of moral consistency as the absence of contradictions in a person's moral living. Everyone is called to live a life without contradiction, both performative and existential. What a person knows to be true or right to do, should not contradict his/her existential living. This is the hallmark of ethics. Ethics is supposed to provide a person with a guide for moral living, and to do so the guide must be rational, and to be rational it must be free of contradictions. We need to constantly evaluate our beliefs, our values and our actions.

Chapter two helped us to understand that knowing is not a 'one single event'. It is a process which involves several acts. Knowing is not synonymous with looking or sensing. It starts with sense data, and moves on to the muscling of insights, the weighing of evidence and culminates in judgment. It is at the fourth level of deliberating that we have to make a choice. And it is here that we need to avoid a contradiction between what we *know* and how we *ought* to live.

Chapter three focused on one of the most popular and important principles in moral thinking and acting – the Golden Rule. It is generally viewed as the principle of treating others as we want to be treated ourselves. But this general formulation is not complete. It gives only the literal meaning of the principle. The proper formulation, as proposed by Gensler, is, "Treat others only as you consent to being treated in the same situation." The addition of "in the same situation" reveals the true meaning of the Rule. People have applied the literal meaning without asking themselves whether they were in "the same situation". When Golden Rule is well articulated and well applied, the result is sufficient moral consistency.

In our thinking about moral issues, there is one faculty that is very vital – conscience. Conscience is a faculty (in the intellect) of moral judgment that distinguishes between right and wrong. We identified various types of consciences and we understood their differences. We should only act when our conscience is clear. Our conscience can be in conflict with the will, but when we let our conscience be overruled by the will, then we enter into moral inconsistency.

We next explored the possible foundations of our moral conscience. Most of the religious traditions trace the foundation of moral conscience to the natural law. According to St. Thomas Aquinas, the natural law contains the basic principles of practical rationality for the human person and the precepts of the natural law that are universally knowable and binding by nature. If this is true, then no one can claim to be exempt from the natural law.

Most of us would agree that we have free will, but what exactly this term means is not clear to many. Birds of the air seem to enjoy some freedom as they soar in the sky. But can they be termed "responsible" for what they do? For sure, it would be ridiculous to "reprimand" a bird for 'deliberately' depositing its droppings on a plate of food. But if a person did something similar, he/she would be deemed responsible for his/her behavior. This is simply because it is only the human person who is endowed with rationality.

GENERAL CONCLUSION

Can a person be so biased in his/her moral thinking that it leads him/her to defective actions? This is a real possibility. We are all prone to bias. Our moral horizons vary from person to person. Our upbringings are different. Our educations vary. Our social experiences differ. Our religious backgrounds are not the same. We are engaged in different dramas of life. There is a dialectic tension within us. And so, we can expect biases to occur. And if biases are not identified and corrected, they can easily result in moral inconsistency.

"Dialectic" deals with conflicts brought about by bias. There is a possibility of eliminating (or at least reducing) biases. Lonergan explains clearly how biases can be eradicated by the process of conversion. There are three kinds of conversion: intellectual, moral and religious. It is only total conversion that can bring about authentic moral consistency.

But one important existential question which the modern man/woman asks is, "Is there a goal to aim at when struggling for more perfection?" A possible answer to this question is "happiness". Each day people everywhere are struggling to find some kind of some fulfilment. People want to be happy in their moral living. Chapter nine discusses the meaning of happiness from the historical perspective. In the final analysis, the truth is that people are happier and more fulfilled when they live consistent moral lives.

But when people discover that they are not satisfied with their constant striving for more and more happiness, then the question of God may emerge. Is the struggle for moral consistency in vain? Is there anything beyond the sensible? The last chapter helped us to appreciate that the human person has the capacity for self-transcendence. This is the search for the divine and it leads to what Lonergan calls religious experience. We need to have an authentic religious experience in order to live free, rational and responsible moral lives. We need to achieve authentic moral consistency.

Bibliography

Primary Sources (Lonergan Books)

Bernard LONERGAN, *Insight: A Study of Human Understanding*, Edited by Frederick E. Crowe and Robert M. Doran, Collected Works of Bernard Lonergan, vol. 3. Toronto: Toronto University Press, 1992. First Published by Longmans, Green and Co. in 1957.

_____. *Understanding and Being: The Halifax Lectures on Insight*. Collected Works of Bernard Lonergan, vol. 5. Edited by Elizabeth A. Morelli and Mark D. Morelli, revised and augmented by Frederick E. Crowe with the collaboration of Elizabeth A. Morelli, Mark D. Morelli, Robert M. Doran, and Thomas V. Daly. Toronto: University of Toronto Press, 1990.

_____. *A Second Collection*, Collected Works of Bernard Lonergan, vol. 13, edited by Robert M. Doran and John D. Dadosky. Toronto: University of Toronto Press, 2016.

_____. *A Third Collection*, Collected Works of Bernard Lonergan, vol. 16, edited by Robert M. Doran and John D. Dadosky. Toronto: University of Toronto Press, 2017.

_____. *Grace and Freedom: Operative Grace in the Thought of St. Thomas Aquinas*, Edited by Frederick E. Crowe and Robert M. Doran, Collected Works of Bernard Lonergan, vol. 1. Toronto: University of Toronto Press, 2000.

_____. *Method in Theology*. Toronto: University of Toronto Press, 1972.

Lonergan: Secondary Source, Books

BYRNE, Patrick H. *The Ethics of Discernment: Lonergan's Foundations for Ethics*. Toronto: University of Toronto Press, 2017.

CRONIN, Brian. *Foundations of Philosophy: Lonergan's Cognitional Theory and Epistemology*. Nairobi: Consolata Institute of Philosophy, 1999.

DORAN, Robert M. *Theology and Dialectics of History*. Toronto: University of Toronto Press, 1990.

_____. *Subject and Psyche*. Milwaukee Wisconsin: Marquette University Press. 1994.

Fellows of the Woodstock Theological Center. *The Realms of Desire: An Introduction to the Thought of Bernard Lonergan*. Washington DC: Woodstock Theological Center, 2011.

FLANAGAN, Joseph. *Quest for Self-Knowledge: An Essay in Lonergan's Philosophy*. Toronto: Toronto University Press, 1997.

GREGSON, V. ed. *The desires of the Human heart: An Introduction to the Theology of Bernard Lonergan*. New York: Paulist Press, 1988.

TEKIPPE, Terry J. *An Introductory Guide to Insight*. New York: Paulist Press, 2003.

_____. *What is Lonergan up to in Insight?* Collegeville: The Liturgical Press, 1996.

TYRRELL, Bernard. *Bernard Lonergan's Philosophy of God*. Dublin: Gill and Macmillan, 1974.

Lonergan: Secondary Source, Articles

AMOUR, Paul. "Bernard Lonergan on Affirmation of the Existence of God." *Analecta Hermeneutica, Vol. 2*. 2010.

GREGSON, V. "The Desire to Know: Intellectual Conversion." *The Desires of the Human Heart: An Introduction to the Theology of Bernard Lonergan.* New York: Paulist Press, 1988.

TYRELL, Bernard. "Passages and Conversions." in *Creativity and Method: Essays in Honor of Bernard Lonergan.* Ed. Matthew L. Lamb. Milwaukee: Marquette University Press, 1981.

Other Books

AQUINAS, Thomas. *Summa Theologica.*

_____. *III Contra Gentes.*

_____. *Treatise on Law* ed. Stanley Parry. Chicago: Henry Regnery Company, 1969.

ARISTOTLE, Rhetoric, Book I

_____. *The Nicomachean Ethics*

BABCOCK Gove, Philip ed. *Webster's Third New International Dictionary.* Springfield: G & C Merrian Company, 1969.

BARTLETT, Aristotle. R. C., & Collins, S. D. *Aristotle's Nicomachean Ethics.* Chicago: University of Chicago Press, 2011.

BENTHAM, Jeremy. *An Odyssey of Ideas*, ed. Mary P. Mack. London: Heineman Publishers, 1962.

BENTLEY HART, David. *The Experience of God: Being, Consciousness, Bliss.* London: Yale University Press, 2013.

BERLIN, Isaiah. *The Root of Romanticism*, (2nd ed.) Princeton: Princeton University Press, 2013.

CICERO, *De Legibus*, bk. 1

CLARKE, Randolph. *Libertarian Accounts of Free Will.* Oxford: Oxford University Press, 2003.

COHEN, G. A. *Lectures of the History of Moral and Political Philosophy.* Jonathan Wolff, ed. New Jersey: Princeton University Press, 2014.

DAWKINS, Richard. *The God Delusion.* New York: Houghton Mifflin Harcourt, 2006.

DESCARTES, Rene. *Passions of the Soul.* Indiana: Hackett Publishing Company, n.d.

FISCHER, John Martin and Mark Ravizza. *Responsibility and Control: A Theory of Moral Responsibility.* Cambridge: Cambridge University Press 1998.

FLANNERY, Kevin L. *Action & Character According to Aristotle.* Washington DC: The Catholic University of America Press, 2013.

GENSLER, Harry J. *Ethics: A Contemporary Introduction.* London: Routledge Publishers, 2011.

_____., *Ethics and the Golden Rule.* London: Routledge Publishers, 2013.

HOMERIN, Emil and Neusner, Jacob eds. *The Golden Rule: The Ethics of Reciprocity in World Religions.* Bloomsbury: Bloomsbury Publishing Press, 2008.

KREEFT, Peter. *Ethics: a History of Modern Thought.* Boston: Recorded Books LLC, 2003.

LUGIRA, Aloysius M. edited by Joanne O'Brien and Martin Palmer. *African Tradition Religion,* New York: Chelsea House Publishers, 2009.

MBITI, John S. *African Religions and Philosophy.* New York: Doubleday & Company, Inc., 1969.

PEREBOOM, Derk. *Living Without Free Will.* Cambridge: Cambridge University Press, 2001.

PLATO, *Phaedo* in the *Portraits of Socrates,* Sir R.W. Livingstone trans. New York: Oxford University Press, 1963.

_____. *Euthyphro.*

BIBLIOGRAPHY

_____. *Giogias*.

_____. *The Republic*.

_____. *Symposium*.

SAHAKIAN, William S. *History of Philosophy: From the Earliest to the Present*. New York: Barnes and Noble Books, 1968.

SEDGWICK, Sally. *Kant's Groundwork of the Metaphysics of Morals: An Introduction*, Cambridge: Cambridge University Press, 2008.

SINAG-TALA, *Conscience and Freedom, 2nd Edition*. Manila: 1992.

STENGER, Victor. *God: The Failed Hypothesis: How Science Shows That God Does Not Exist*. New York: Prometheus, 2008.

"Transcript of the Russell/Copleston Radio Debate". Philosophy of Religion.

ULEMAN, Jennifer K. *An Introduction to Kant's Moral Philosophy*. Cambridge: Cambridge University Press, 2010.

WILSON, John A. *The Culture of Ancient Egypt*. Chicago: University of Chicago Press, 1956.

Other Articles

FLEW, Antony *ed.* "Golden Rule" in *A Dictionary of Philosophy*. London: The MacMillan Press, 1979.

RAMOSE, Mogobe B. "The Ethics of Ubuntu." *The African Philosophy Reader*, Second Edition, eds. P.H. Coetzee and A.P.J. Roux. New York: Routledge, 2003.

METZ, Thaddeus and Gaie, Joseph B.R. "The African ethic of Ubuntu/Botho: Implications for Research on Morality." *Journal of Moral Education* 39, 2010.

METZ, Thaddeus. "Toward an African Moral Theory," *The Journal of Political Philosophy 15(3)* 2007.

GALEN, Strawson. "Freedom and Belief." *Philosophical Studies*, 75. Oxford: Clarendon Press, 1986.

NIELSEN, Kai. "God and the Basis of Morality." *The Journal of Religious Ethics, Vol. 10, No. 2* (Fall, 1982).

APPENDIX

You can consult the appendix (53 pages) of this book here

Or in the digital version on the Immatériel platform www.immateriel.fr or send an email to commandes@domunipress.fr.

INDEX

Acknowledgment 7
Foreword 9
General Introduction 15
I. Moral Consistency: A Short Historical Exploration 21
    The Sophistry Period: The Inauguration of the Era of Free Choice..... 23
    Socrates: Knowledge as Virtue 24
    Aristotle: The Principle of Self-Destruction 26
    St. Thomas Aquinas: Virtue as a Good Quality of the Mind 27
    Immanuel Kant: The Activity of Human Will 28
    African Conception of Morality 30
    Bernard Lonergan: Self-Appropriation 38
    Lonergan's Contribution 44
    Concluding Remarks and Suggestions 45
    Case Study 1: The Question of Identity 46
II. Thinking, Knowing and Objectivity 49
    Part I: Cognitional Theory (Thinking) 50
    The Term 'Cognition' 50
    The Eureka Experience 51
    How an Insight Emerges 57
    Higher Viewpoints 58
    Inverse Insights 59
    Heuristic Structure 61
    Part II: Epistemology (knowing) and Objectivity 62
    Making a Transition 62
    Human Beings Desire to Know 62
    The Virtually Unconditioned 64
    Correctness of Insights into Concrete Situation 66
    Self-Affirmation of the Knower 68
    The Notion of Consciousness 69
    Three levels of Consciousness 69
    The Unity of Consciousness 69
    Self-affirmation 70
    The Impossibility of Revision 71
    The Notion of Objectivity 72

  Case Study 2: Reporting on the Death of Gerald 78

III. The Golden Rule 81
  The Golden Rule in the Twelve Religions of the World 82
  Seven Variations (or Relatives) of the Golden Rule 83
  Socrates and the Golden Rule 84
  Golden Rule and Role-Taking 85
  Kant's Objection of the Golden Rule 85
  The Golden Rule Promotes Good, not Evil 86
  The Golden Rule and Altruism 87
  Gensler's Formulation of the Golden Rule 88
  Lonergan and the Golden Rule 93
  Lonergan's Contribution 94
  Concluding Remarks and Suggestions 94
  Case Study 3: "Mercy Killing" 95

IV. The Notion of Conscience 97
  The Etymology of the Word "Conscience" 98
  Synderesis 98
  Seven Types of Consciences 99
  The Formation of Conscience 101
  Some Normative Underpinnings of Conscience 106
  Lonergan: On Conscience 108
  Lonergan's Contribution 112
  Concluding Remarks and Suggestions 112
  Case Study 4: False Witness 113

V. The Natural Law 115
  Historical Exploration 116
  The Idea of Natural Goodness 120
  Transition from "the good" to "the right" 122
  Lonergan: A New Approach to Natural Law 124
  Lonergan's Contribution 130
  Concluding Remarks and Suggestions 130
  Case Study 5: Same Sex Marriage 131

VI. Freedom and Responsibility 133
  Analogous Meanings of the Word 'Freedom' 134
  The Notion of Freedom in Lonergan 135
  Lonergan's Contribution 147
  Concluding Remarks and Suggestions 148
  Case Study 6: Free will vs Duty 149

VII. The Four-fold Bias 151

    Dramatic Bias 152
    Individual Bias 155
    Group Bias 157
    General Bias 159
    Lonergan's Contribution 161
    Concluding Remarks and Suggestions 162
    Case Study 7: Legislators 163

VIII. A Call to Conversion 165
    Conflicts 166
    Horizons 167
    Conversions 168
    Intellectual Conversion 169
    Religious Conversion 170
    Moral Conversion 171
    Lonergan's Contribution 174
    Concluding Remarks and Suggestions 174
    Case Study 8: Harassment by Senior Officer 175

IX. The Notion of Happiness 177
    All Human Beings Naturally Desire Happiness
    Socrates (c. 470 – c. 399 BCE) 178
    The Reason, the Will and the Desire
    Plato (c. 428 – c. 347 BCE) 180
    Happiness Results from the Cultivation of Virtue
    Aristotle (384 – 322 BCE) 180
    Pleasure of the Mind brings True Happiness
    Epicurus (c. 341 – c. 270 BCE) 182
    The Good Flow of Life - Stoicism 184
    God as the Highest Good
    St. Thomas Aquinas (1225–1274) 184
    The Intellectual Love of God as the Highest Happiness
    Rene Descartes (1596 – 1650) 185
    Happiness as "True Pleasure"
    John Locke (1632-1704) 186
    Utilitarianism as the Greatest Happiness
    Jeremy Bentham (1748 – 1832) 186
    Self-actualization as the Highest Happiness
    Abraham Maslow (1908 – 1970) 187
    "The Good" for the Highest Happiness: Lonergan (1904 – 1984) 188
    Lonergan's Contribution 195
    Concluding Remarks and Suggestions 195
    Case Study 9: Unfulfilled life of Malaren 196

X. The Question of God 199
   African Religious Experience and the Question of God 200
   Ontological Arguments for the Existence of God 203
   Malcom's Modal Version of the Anselm's Ontological Argument ... 205
   Criticisms and Objections of Ontological Argument 206
   The Five Ways of St. Thomas Aquinas 208
   A Short Critique of the "Five Ways" 210
   Some Responses in Defense of the "Five Ways" 211
   Lonergan and Aquinas: A Critique of Aquinas's Method 215
   The Reality of God: Bernard Lonergan 216
   Morality and the Question of God 225
   Lonergan's Contribution 227
   Concluding Remarks and Suggestions 228
   Case Study 10: Freud vs Lewis 228

General Conclusion 231

Bibliography 235

DOMUNI-PRESS
publishing house of DOMUNI University

« Le livre grandit avec le lecteur »
"The book grows with the reader."

The University

Domuni University was founded in 1999 by French Dominicans. It offers Bachelor, Master and Doctorate degrees by distance learning, as well as "à la carte" (stand-alone) courses and certificates in philosophy, theology, religious sciences, and social sciences (including both state and canonical diplomas). It welcomes several thousand students on its teaching platform, which operates in five languages: French, English, Spanish, Italian, and Arabic. The platform is accompanied by more than three hundred professors and tutors. Anchored in the Order of Preachers, Domuni University benefits from its centuries-old tradition of study and research. Innovative in many ways, Domuni consists of an international network that offers courses to students worldwide.

To find out more about Domuni:
www.domuni.eu

The publishing house

Domuni-Press disseminates research and publishes works in the academic fields of interest of Domuni University: theology, philosophy, spirituality, history, religions, law and social sciences. Domuni-Press is part of a lively research community located at the heart of the Dominican network. Domuni-Press aims to bring readers closer to their texts by making it possible, via the help of today's digital technology, to have immediate access to them, while ensuring a quality paperback edition. Each work is published in both forms. The key word is simplicity. The subjects are approached with a clear editorial line: academic quality, accessible to all, with the aim of spreading the richness of Christian thought. Six collections are available: theology, philosophy, spirituality, Bible, history, law and social sciences. Domuni-Press has its own online bookshop: www.domunipress.fr. Its books are also available on its main distance selling website: Amazon, Fnac.com, and in more than 900 bookshops and sales outlets around the world.

To find out more about the publishing house:
www.domunipress.fr

EXTRACT FROM THE CATALOGUE

Jean-François ARNOUX,
Et le désert refleurira.

Sabine GINALHAC,
Désir d'enfant. L'éclairage inattendu des récits bibliques.

Pierrette FUZAT,
Un nom au bout de la nuit. Le combat de Jacob.

Patrice SABATER,
La terre en Palestine/Israël.

Marie MONNET,
Emmanuel Levinas. La relation à l'autre.

Apollinaire KIVYAMUNDA,
Maurice Zundel, une biographie spirituelle.

Juliette BORDES,
Viens Colombe. Saint Jean de la Croix.

Joseph MARTY,
Christianisme et Cinéma.

Michel VAN AERDE,
Le père retrouvé

Monique-Lise COHEN, Marie-Thérèse DESOUCHE,
Emmanuel Levinas et la pensée de l'infini.

Claire REGGIO,
Le christianisme des premiers siècles.

Ameer JAJE,
Diaconesses. Les femmes dans l'Église syriaque.

Jean-Paul COUJOU (sous la direction de),
L'État et le pouvoir.

Françoise DUBOST,
L'Évangile des animaux.

Markus JOST,
   La Bible à l'école d'Ignace de Loyola et de Menno Simons.

Paul TAVARDON, ocso,
   Trappistes en terre sainte. Des moines au cœur de la géopolitique. Latroun, 1890-1946 (T.1).

Paul TAVARDON, ocso,
   Trappistes en terre sainte. Des moines au cœur de la géopolitique. Latroun, 1946-1991 (T.2).

Marie MONNET (sous la direction de),
   La source théologique du droit.

Nilson Léal DE SA,
   La vie fraternelle.

Apollinaire KIVYAMUNDA,
   Maurice Zundel. La relation à Dieu.

Lara LOYE,
   Fraternités.

Bernadette ESCAFFRE,
   Vocations. Quand Dieu appelle.

Raphaël HAAS,
   Pleine conscience. Bouddhisme et christianisme en dialogue.

Augustin WILIWOLI,
   Axel Honneth. Lutter pour la reconnaissance.

Louis FROUART,
   Pascal. Cœur, Corps, Esprit.

Emmanuel BOISSIEU,
   Platon. Une manière de vivre.

Emmanuel BOISSIEU,
   Kant. Une philosophie de la liberté.

Marie MONNET,
   Dieu migrant.

Thérèse HEBBELINCK,
   L'Église catholique et les juifs (T.1 et T.2).

Béatrice PAPASOGLOU,
  Qu'est-ce que l'homme ?

Augustin WILIWOLI SIBILONI op,
  Ce que les philosophes disent du vivre-ensemble.

François MENAGER,
  Yves Bonnefoy, poète et philosophe.

Nicole AWAIS,
  L'art d'enseigner le fait religieux.

Thérèse M. ANDREVON,
  Une théologie à la frontière (T.1 et T2).

Michel VAN AERDE,
  Venez vous reposer. Antidotes spirituels au burn-out.

Agnès GODEFROY,
  Bien vieillir, dans les pas d'Abraham.

Olivier BELLEIL,
  Résolution des conflits dans l'Église primitive.

Anton MILH op & Stephan VAN ERP,
  Identité et visibilité. Conflits de générations chez les Dominicains.

Denis LABOURE,
  Astrologie et religion au Moyen Age.

Jorel FRANÇOIS,
  Voltaire, philosophe de la religion.

Augustin WILIWOLI SIBILONI op,
  La reconnaissance. Réparer les blessures.

Jean Baptiste ZEKE,
  Loi naturelle et post-humanisme.

Emmanuel BOISSIEU,
  Paul Ricœur. Un inconditionnel de l'amour.

Ameer JAJE,
  Le chiisme. Clés historiques et théologiques.

Jean-René PEGGARY,
  L'aube d'une pensée américaine. L'individu chez H. D. Thoreau.

Jean-François ARNOUX,
  Comme un feu dévorant. Flammèches d'une lecture incarnée de la Bible.

Olivier BELLEIL,
  L'autre dans l'islam coranique.

Sœur Agnès DE LA CROIX,
  Miroir juif des évangiles.

Jean-Michel COSSE,
  Au centre de l'âme.

Jean-Paul BALDAZZA,
  Antoine. Un saint d'Orient et d'Occident.

Ameer JAJE,
  Marie dans l'islam.

Olivier PERRU,
  Le corps malade.

Jesmond MICALLEF,
  Trinitarian Ontology.

Abel TOE,
  Pauvreté et développement au Burkina-Faso.

Jude Thaddeus MBI AKEM,
  Le développement en Afrique.

Claude LICHTERT,
  Lire la Bible ensemble.

Jorel FRANÇOIS,
  Voltaire, philosophe contre le fanatisme.

Bruno CALLEBAUT,
  Les Évangiles. Leurs origines, leurs exégèses.

Claude LICHTERT,
  La parole pour sortir de soi. Dieu et les humains aujourd'hui : parcours biblique.

Heriberto CABRERA REYES,
Effondrement, apocalypse ou renaissance ? Théologie en temps de crise.

Patrick MONJOU,
Comment prêcher à la fin du Moyen Âge ? (T. 1 et T. 2).

Robert PLÉTY,
À la découverte du Rabbi de Nazareth (T. 1).

Robert PLÉTY,
À la rencontre du Rabbi de Nazareth (T. 2).

Jules KATSURANA,
Guide pour la Prévention de la violence sexiste.

Jacques FOURNIER,
La Trinité, mystère d'amour.

Louis D'HÉROUVILLE,
Marie-Madeleine, femme pascale.

Olivier PERRU,
Martin-Stanislas Gillet (1875-1951). La peur de l'effort intellectuel.

Paul-Marcel LEMAIRE,
Vivre l'Évangile.

John Jack LYNCH,
Judith, Sarah and Esther. Jewish heroines.

François FAURE,
Emmanuel Mounier : La personne est son engagement (T. 1).

François FAURE,
Emmanuel Mounier : Montrer, sans démontrer (T. 2).

www.ingramcontent.com/pod-product-compliance
Lightning Source LLC
Chambersburg PA
CBHW071710180426
43192CB00053B/2249